DARIEN

The Death and Rebirth
of a Southern Town

DARIEN

The Death and Rebirth
of a Southern Town

by
Spencer B. King, Jr.

illustrated by
Irene Dodd

Mercer University
Press
Macon, Ga. 31207

ISBN 0-86554-003-9   MUP/H006

Darien.
The Death and Rebirth of a Southern Town.
Copyright ©1981
Mercer University Press, Macon, Georgia 31210-3960
All rights reserved
Printed in the United States of America

The paper used in this publication meets the minimum requirements
of American National Standard for Information Sciences—
Permanence of Paper for Printed Library Materials, ANSI Z39.48–1984.

Library of Congress Cataloging-in-Publication Data

King, Spencer Bidwell, 1904–1977
Darien : the death and rebirth of a southern town.
Bibliography : p. 105.
Includes index.
1. Darien, Ga.—History—Civil War, 1861–1865.
2. Darien, Ga.—History.
I. Title.
F294.D26K56   973.7'09758'737   80-83662
ISBN 0-86554-003-9

Contents

To my Children

I have made
a ceaseless effort
not to ridicule,
not to bewail,
nor to scorn human actions,
but to understand them.

—Spinoza

List of Illustrations

Spencer B. King, Jr.

FOREWORD

Spencer Bidwell King, Jr.
1904-1977

Although born in Birmingham, Alabama, Mercer University and Georgia were the focal points of Spencer Bidwell King's life and career. He graduated from Mercer in 1929 and returned in 1946 as chairman of the Department of History, a position he held until 1970. He was a major force in the growth and expansion of the department to its present size and helped to impart to the department its special identity both in and outside the University.

Professor King was an indefatigable worker and over the years published innumerable books, articles, and newspaper columns. All of Southern history was his domain but Georgia history was his special love, his best known work being *Georgia Voices* (1966). The present study of the destruction of Darien began many years ago as a relatively short article and over the years evolved to its present form. He would doubtless have continued his work on this topic that held such fascination for him had his career not been cut short by his death.

Professor King was the prototype of the kind, thoughtful gentleman. He possessed a special gift for transfusing his enthusiasm for Southern history to others and innumerable students left his classes filled with an abiding interest in Southern history and culture. Professor King's death in 1977 after an extended illness constituted a great loss for the University, the historical profession, his family and his many friends.

—Henry Y. Warnock
Mercer University
October, 1980

PREFACE

ALTHOUGH THIS story of real people and actual events of the past century moves away from its center, some times as far away as Kansas Territory and again as far away as Boston, the seat of New England abolitionism, it focuses on Darien, Georgia, where most of the action takes place. And as measured in time, although the climax is reached in June, 1863, the story goes back first to the origin of Darien and the early settlers on the Altamaha Delta, then moves forward to the bloody days of border warfare in Kansas and to the greater war, and finally beyond the Civil War to a time when memories of sectional hatred had begun to fade.

Some will find in the story the problem of good and evil, a conflict between right and wrong. But there will not be agreement as to what is right and what is wrong. Some will call respect for private property and obedience to law good, while others will say liberty and freedom are more precious than property. The voice of reason will say law and liberty are both virtues. But each of these can become evil if it attempts to negate the other completely.

Some who play their roles here are heroes, some villains, and some neither—just people doing a job. Or people, white and black, living through the hell of war and the agony of radical change. Some represent fanatic crusaders, some courageous humanitarians, some the victims of violence and lawlessness. Let him who wishes decide whom to justify or whom to blame.

The Shaw letters pertaining to the destruction and restoration of Darien were preserved by successive generations until they finally came into the hands of the late John Clarke. Mr. Clarke, who lived on the Ridge beyond Darien, wrote me before his death saying he had loaned the letters to a reporter on *The Atlanta Constitution*. The reporter was killed "in a row of some kind" and editor Clark Howell was unable to recover them. Fortunately, copies of the letters were passed down through the family of William Robert Gignilliat, senior warden of St. Andrews at the time of its burning and during the period of the building of the chapel on the Ridge. Those copies came into the hands of William's grandson, Thomas H. Gignilliat, an attorney-at-law in Savannah. It was through Mr. Gignilliat's cousin, Mrs. Broadus E. Willingham, Junior, of Macon, that I learned of these copies and became interested in the story they tell. The validity of the Gignilliat copies is confirmed by excerpts from them published in *Harper's Weekly* (see Notes).

I am deeply indebted to William G. Haynes and his sister Frances for their interest and helpful suggestions made in the early stages of my writing. Without them many questions in my mind would remain unanswered. Also, Bessie Lewis, an authority on the history of the region, helped me avoid some pitfalls. Another who guided me gently and lovingly around pitfalls relating to the South Carolina coast was my wife, Caroline Paul, who spent her girlhood days in Port Royal and Beaufort.

I am grateful for courtesies shown me by librarians and archivists in Savannah, Atlanta, Athens, Topeka, Boston, and New York City. Professor Henry Y. Warnock, my colleague in the History Department of Mercer University, did me the favor of reading the manuscript. Peggy Watson assisted in the preparation of the index, and Bessie Killebrew patiently typed and retyped the manuscript through its tedious development.

A substantial part of the first chapter appeared in a piece I did on Darien for *The Atlanta Journal-Constitution Magazine*, February 7, 1971.

My thanks to all those named and the unnamed friends. But none of them should bear the burden of errors. That is mine to carry.

Spencer King

I

OF THE TOWN AND THE RIVER

THE FIRE which consumed the Georgia Town of Darien, a small but prosperous village at the mouth of the Altamaha River, on a fateful June day in 1863 when Negro soldiers put the torch to it was the tangible expression of an uncontrolled hate which enveloped the entire nation. That fire burned almost all the homes and public buildings of Darien, including the school and churches, and it engendered a responsive hate that burned in the hearts of the citizens of the town after the red embers had grown cold. This is the story of how that hate began, how it manifested itself in the destruction of Darien, and how passion finally cooled.

The undefended town was almost totally destroyed on June 11, 1863, sacked and burned by Negro troops acting under orders of white officers. There were two principals at the scene of action. Colonel Robert Gould Shaw, the first to be blamed for the evil deed by the local citizens, was from Boston; Colonel James Montgomery, the ranking officer, was from Kansas. Each of these men was in command of a Negro regiment. Shaw commanded the Fifty-Fourth Massachusetts Volunteers, the first military contingent of Northern Negroes to fight for the freedom of their enslaved brothers; and Montgomery commanded the Second South Carolina Volunteers, a regiment composed of slaves taken from the plantations along the fertile Carolina and Georgia coast. Both colonels were under General David Hunter, Union commander of the Southern Department comprising the states of South Carolina, Georgia, and Florida. Hunter's headquarters was on Hilton Head Island on the South

Carolina coast above Savannah. The Darien episode was to bring Shaw and Montgomery together in the burning business. One of these would have to bear the guilt more heavily than the other; but Hunter, their superior, also stands before the bar of historical judgment.

Darien, the focal point of the story, is situated on the northernmost channel of four principal channels making the mouth of the Altamaha River. This picturesque stream, this "other Nile", was of great importance to the economic life of the region.[1] The Altamaha itself is fed by two rivers, the Ocmulgee and the Oconee, that drain the waters of middle and upper Georgia. Thus, Darien of olden times represented in a true sense the life and history of the state; and what happened to Darien in June, 1863, affected Georgians generally, symbolizing the life of the South during the Civil War— a time of healing through bloodletting.

Darien lived by the Grace of God and the River. The Altamaha was her economic and social life line and by the River came also the instrument of her death in the summer of 1863. The Altamaha spreads out through the marshes and empties into the Atlantic ocean between Sapelo and St. Simons, two of Georgia's Golden Isles. Golden, whatever the term may have meant to earlier explorers searching for the precious metal, meant to Sir Robert Montgomery and other early promoters much more than the yellow metal or the beauty of color. Sir Robert Montgomery's *Margravate of Azilia* (1717) is a well-known piece of promotional literature appealing to prospective investors in the land which would eventually be known as Georgia. The appeal was to those who loved beauty and who would be attracted to an almost perfect climate, but withal was the promise of economic gain. Thus, the promoters were interested in profits from investments in a land blessed with natural beauty, warmed by the golden sun, and ready to yield treasures far greater than gold itself.[2] Golden is inadequate to fully describe the marshy lands which inspired Georgia poet Sidney Lanier to marvel at

> A league and a league of marsh-grass,
> waist-high, broad in the blade. . .

----

[1]See E. Merton Coulter, *Thomas Spalding of Sapelo* (Baton Route, 1940), p. 163. Coulter quotes the following verse from the Savannah *Georgia Gazette* (June 3, 1784): "Another Nile remote in Southern climes / and fertile soil, reserv'd for better times; /Whose seven mouths discharge their limpid flood, /on either side where FREDERICA stood."

[2]See Verner W. Crane, *The Promotion Literature of Georgia* (Cambridge, 1925), *The Southern Frontier, 1670-1732* (Ann Arbor, 1956); Burnette Vanstory, *Georgia's Land of Golden Isles* (Athens, 1956).

The sight of it freed Lanier's soul

> From the weighing of fate
> and the sad discussion of sin. . .

The cypress, live oak, and pine made Darien an important lumber center and later a naval stores shipping point. By 1835 the economic life of the town depended upon shipping cargoes of lumber, rice, and cotton. It is said that ante-bellum Darien reached such a peak of activity before the Civil War that sometimes as many as thirty ships arrived and cleared in a day.

The town lies sixty miles below Savannah and twenty miles above Brunswick, both now thriving cities. There was a time in the life of Darien when it appeared that she might become the Queen of Coastal Georgia. In 1818 this town was made the seat of government of McIntosh county whose marshy coast is broken by many bays and inlets, chief of which are Sapelo, Doboy, and Altamaha sounds. From the ocean the channel approach to Darien is through Doboy Sound. That channel is sometimes called the Darien River, but it is really the north branch of the Altamaha. The English had built a fort there before the Georgia colony was founded, but Fort King George, as it was called, was garrisoned by His Majesty's Independent Company for a short time only, from 1721 to 1727.[3] The county gets its name from John McIntosh Mohr, leader of the Scottish settlers whom, along with others, Oglethorpe brought from the Highlands of Scotland in 1736 to defend English America against the Spaniards. The Highlanders left Inverness, their old Scottish homeland, on October 18, 1735, aboard the *Prince of Wales.* They had turned their eyes westward but had not forgotten their Bonnic Scotland,

> Land of brown heath and shaggy wood;
> Land of the mountain and the flood . . .

They had sailed away from the Dee and the Don to settle on the banks of a river bordered not by heather but by marsh grass. George Dunbar, the ship's captain, brought them safely to Georgia in January, 1736. Those bold and hardy Scots rowed up the Altamaha, and on a bluff on the north side of the river they built their town. Captain Dunbar named it Darien. This pleased the Highlanders who, standing guard against their Spanish foes, remembered an earlier venture when their forebears defied Spain's power by attempting to establish in 1698 a settlement on the isthmus now called Panama but known as Darien to the Indians who then inhabited it. Keats, too, remembered that earlier Darien when, "On First Looking Into Chapman's Homer," he wrote

---

[3]The restoration of this fort is under the authority of the Georgia Historical Commission.

> . . . like stout Cortez when with eagle eyes
> He star'd at the Pacific—and all his men
> Look'd at each other with a wild surmise—
> Silent, upon a peak in Darien.

The Spaniards were victorious in the contest for that earlier Darien. This second Darien would not suffer another such fate at the hands of the Spaniards. Its great tragedy would be of another time and at the hands of another foe.[4]

Oglethorpe was well pleased with those sturdy fighters who would drive the Spaniards out of Georgia after their victory over them at Bloody Marsh in 1742; and he was pleased by the healthy growth of the town. Sam Eveleigh noted this:

> I understand that Mr. Oglethorpe is extremely well pleased with the Behaviour of the Scotch Highlanders on Allatomcha [sic] River, Who have already built themselves a Smal Fort and Fourteen Hutts in order to defend themselves from an Enamy, the Cold and Rain, and He wear's Some time amongst them an Highland Habit.[5]

They were vigorous and healthy Scots who peopled Darien. In addition to the McIntosh clan there were the McDonalds, Mackleans, McKays, Munros, McBains, Burges's, Cuthberts, Morrisons, and Clarks. The Reverend John McLeod was their minister and was in charge of the school as well as the kirk.

These people were industrious, no more afraid to work than to fight. Moreover, they were loyal to Oglethorpe and shared with him his opposition to Negro slavery. On January 3, 1739, they drew up a petition setting forth their reasons for objecting to the introduction of slavery, which their Savannah River neighbors were demanding. The reasons given by the eighteen Darien freeholders who signed the petition against slavery were the nearness of the Spaniards who would encourage the slaves to escape to freedom, the fact that, in their opinion, their own people would be "more usefully employed" than the Negroes, and the possible loss of money invested in case of failure to recover a fugitive slave. Finally, the humanitarian reason was given:

> It is shocking to human nature, that any race of mankind
> and their Posterity, should be sentenced to perpetual

---

[4]See Bessie Mary Lewis, "Darien: A Symbol of Defiance and Achievement," *Georgia Historical Quarterly*, XX (Sept., 1936), 185-198.

[5]*Colonial Records of the State of Georgia* (Atlanta, 1910), XXI, 120.

slavery, nor in justice can we think otherwise of it, than that they are thrown amongst us to be our Scourge one day or other for our Sins: and as freedome to them must be as dear to us, what a scene of horrour must it bring about! and the longer it is un-executed, the bloody Scene must be the greater.[6]

It would have appeared ironic to the Darien people, burned out by Negroes bent on destroying slavery by force in 1863, if they had remembered that the original settlers had tried to prevent the introduction of Negro slavery into the colony in its early days.

Settlers continued to come to the young town. Among them were the Gignilliats, the Brailsfords, and the Kells. And there was James McGillivray Troup. He was the brother of George McIntosh Troup, Georgia's fiery governor. James Troup's home was built by the leading architect of the period, William Jay, who also did some of Savannah's finest houses. Thomas Spalding was the great-grandson of old John McIntosh Mohr, the original leader of the settlement. Spalding, who owned the Island of Sapelo, was also especially interested in Darien and was its first leading citizen and chief promoter.[7] He built his Darien home about two miles east of the town, far enough out to have missed the flames of destruction in 1863. He called it Ashantilly, after his family's estate in Scotland.[8]

After the Trustees had relinquished their charter and Georgia had become a crown colony the doors to slavery were then thrown wide open and many Carolina planters moved into the younger colony establishing plantations, particularly in the Altamaha Delta. A hundred years before the war that destroyed slavery and Darien with it, South Carolinians established plantations in the Altamaha Delta. In 1820 some of these families were still there. One finds listed in the Fourth United States Census, William Fulton, William Flemming, John McClelland, and William Middleton among the descendants of families which had migrated from South Carolina before the American Revolution. Thomas Butler King of Massachusetts came in 1823. He married Anna Matilda Page the next year and became the owner of her father's estate, "Retreat," on St. Simons Island. This successful planter had become one of Georgia's leading citizens by the time the state seceded from

---

[6]Egmont Papers, Vol. 14203, pp. 368-369, in the University of Georgia Libraries, Athens, Georgia.

[7]See Coulter, *Thomas Spalding*, pp. 162-189.

[8]Ashantilly is now the home of William C. Haynes, publisher of The Ashantilly Press.

the Union, and during the war that followed the Governor sent him as a minister to European capitals. Other big planters well established in the Delta were John Couper, James Hamilton, Dr. Robert Grant, William Brailsford, and Major Pierce Butler. Major Butler owned Butler's Island, one of the most valuable rice plantations, and produced cotton at Hampton Point. More than six hundred slaves worked those two plantations. His wife was a Middleton and his grandson, who took his name, married Frances Anne Kemble, the popular English actress, and brought her to his coastal empire where she lived a short and unhappy existence. Although married to Butler for fifteen years, she lived on his Georgia plantation only briefly at the end of the 1830's. Such an incompatible marriage would inevitably end, and so Fanny finally freed herself from her slave-owning husband.

Roswell King, a native of Connecticut who managed Butler's plantations, moved to north Georgia before the Civil War and founded Roswell near the present city of Atlanta. His brother, Reuben King, a tanner by trade, followed him to Darien at the turn of the nineteenth century and rose to the position of an affluent slave owner and planter. He remained in McIntosh County, living through the trying time of war and witnessing the raid on his Mallow plantation, sixteen miles from the town which had honored him by electing him an alderman in 1822.

Nature had abundantly provided for the land watered by the Altamaha, both in things of beauty to enrich the soul and in the practical things by which man makes his living. Fanny Kemble found an abundance of ducks, geese, and turkeys to supply her table and such domestic animals as cattle, sheep, and pigs. Deer were plentiful in the forest and venison made a good balance for a table loaded with sea food. Fanny learned of hawks and turkey buzzards, and she was especially fond of the mockingbirds. To frighten her, however, there were the centipedes, and to irritate her the fleas "and other still less agreeable vermin." The silver grey moss dripping from the live oaks made a beautiful sight, but had practical use also. The Negroes gathered it and sold it to the people of Darien for mattresses, sofas, and love-seats. Fanny thought the moss was "better than any other material" for such things because it was "as light as horse-hair, as springy and elastic and a great deal less harsh and rigid."[9]

Fanny spoke warmly of the magnolia bay and the wild myrtle, but the "pride of the South" was the *magnolia grandiflora* with its "queenly" blossoms. Thomas Wentworth Higginson, the New England writer and

---

[9]Frances Ann Kemble, *Journal of a Residence on a Georgia Plantation in 1838-1839* (New York, 1863), pp. 20-37.

reformer who commanded a regiment of South Carolina Negroes in their fight for freedom, thought Thomas Butler King's plantation had "the loveliest garden" he had ever seen.[10] Later, another observer wrote: "On one hand woods of pine, oak and cedar grew close to the waterside, while the sea-green, faintly rippled channel was bordered on the other by a world of yellow marsh, beyond which the sea islands were dreams of lilac against the sky."[11]

It was to this beautiful spot—Sir Robert Montgomery had once likened it to Paradise—that Reuben King came at the dawn of the nineteenth century. And it was here that he, like others, found the opportunity to make his living and where, until the flame of hate temporarily scorched the earth, he and William Brailsford, who owned Broughton Island, and all the new neighbors who migrated from near and far found a veritable Garden of Eden.

When Reuben King arrived at Darien in March, 1801, he found only three stores and "about eight dwelling houses."[12] By the time the white Abolitionist officers ordered their Negro soldiers to loot and burn the town it had grown tenfold. At the beginning Reuben King was very busy working with his hands at many jobs—when he was not busy trying every remedy known to man to recover from malaria. Among the "cures" tried by this Yankee victim of a Southern malady were sweet weed tea, pepper and water, fever and ague root, wild cherry tree bark in water, tartar, jallop, and sulphur and rum. He even tried running up and down stairs to break his fever.

As tanning was his trade, it is to be expected that Reuben would cut and peel oak trees and pile the bark ready for the tanning vat. The vat itself had to be constructed before the tanning process could be carried out. Reuben's diary is filled with comments about how many trees he and his neighbors cut, skinned, and sunned. He also planted "mulbury" trees, cut away bushes for a cow pen, rafted timber down the river to build a "tan" house, and cut rafters for it. He helped his brother Roswell make brick and he "hoed" corn. He helped construct boats. He frequently went fishing and often spoke of going after oysters. He hunted and "traveled the woods after nuts." He helped his brother underpin his house and sell his beef. On Saturday, December 5, 1801, "We cleared away a place for a wharf"; on Tuesday, January 5, 1802, he

---

[10]Quoted in Caroline Cooper Lovell, *The Golden Isles of Georgia* (Boston, 1932), p. 258.

[11]*Ibid.*, pp. 21-22.

[12]Reuben King's Journal (MS), The Georgia Historical Society Collection: "The Reuben King Journal, 1801-1806," edited by Virginia Steele Wood and Ralph Van Wood, *The Georgia Historical Quarterly*, L. (1966), 177-206, 296-335, 421-458; LI (1967), 78-120; Spencer King, *Georgia Voices* . . . (Athens, 1966), 161-162.

"made a pair of haims [hames]"; and on Wednesday, February 24, he worked on "a fishing flat" [boat]. On Thursday of that week he helped put in timbers and caulk the boat, and on Friday "We finished it and put it in to the water." On that same day they "sot out some cabbages." On Thursday, April 1, Roswell went to Doboy Sound for oysters while Reuben "halled" wood. We find Reuben helping his brother finish a chimney on April 15, and the next day he began to make a pair of shoes. On Sunday, May 23, he "drawled" off a barrel of molasses for Roswell, and on the 25th went up Cathead Creek for some "hicery" timber for "coggs to the barck wheel."

Some of the Darien people looked upon Reuben King, a Connecticut Yankee, as representative of a strange breed. His thriftiness and industriousness were not understood by some of the reckless young men who frequented the town bars more than they applied themselves to rewarding pursuits. All such small towns of that period had plenty of that sort, but there were enough of the other sort who shared this Yankee's drive and ambition to make the town prosper. They used their energy and initiative and whatever nature provided in that place to meet their daily needs. Through hard work and by working together they were able to build their homes and provide such comforts of home as were possible at the time. Work and cooperation, as well as competition, brought them success and made their town grow. River traffic expanded and economic activity increased.

Rice was a very important cargo for the barges and boats on the Altamaha in the early days of Darien's life. "Oasis," which became the property of James Nephew, the son-in-law of James Gignilliat, was one of the rice plantations. The Altamaha Delta had many such plantations, and "Butler Island," "Hopeton," "Elizafield," "Broadfield," and "New Hope" were familiar place names to the people of the river. Coastal society in which the rice planters moved included the Grants, Butlers, Kings, Wyllys, Troups, Dents, Brailsfords, and Coupers.[13] Cargoes of rice, the most valuable cash crop of the river plantations, were unloaded at Darien and stored in tabby-walled warehouses until re-shipped to market. These buildings were made of oyster shells, sand, and lime, the lime being made from burning the shells.

Darien's economic growth by the time it became the seat of government of McIntosh county was sufficient to cause the legislature to locate a state bank there. The Bank of Darien was chartered on December 15, 1818. The state was allowed to buy five thousand of the ten thousand shares at $100 each, and

---

[13]See Albert V. House, editor, *Planter Management and Capitalism in Ante-Bellum Georgia: The Journal of Hugh Fraser Grant, Ricegrower* (New York, 1954), pp. 5, 13.

fifteen hundred shares were allotted to Darien. Thomas Spalding and four other men of McIntosh County were chosen to open the subscription books there. E. Merton Coulter, in his biography of Spalding, says the bank opened on April 26, 1819, ". . . with high hopes of the town of Darien and of the bank that the commerce of the western and southwestern parts of the state would be drawn down the Altamaha to Darien and thence distributed to the ends of the earth."[14] Spalding was elected president of the bank which was said to have been the strongest financial institution south of Philadelphia. It had branches in a number of Georgia cities and its influence was felt throughout the South.

An indication of the increasing importance of Darien and its social and cultural development is the fact that in 1818, the year it was made the county-seat of McIntosh and got its bank, its first newspaper was established. It was named the Darien *Gazette*. Although it lived only a few years, another, the Darien *Telegraph*, took up the task of reporting the news—slanting its political news toward the Union party, announcing the social events, and carrying advertising notices for the merchants.[15] Two other papers, the *Phoenix* and *The McIntosh County Herald*, each had a short run before the Civil War.[16]

Being high on the bluff overlooking the Darien branch of the Altamaha River the town provided a grand vista. Its citizens could look eastward and see the green cassena bushes and the fan-like palmettoes reaching their pointed fingers toward the gray moss dripping from the limbs of the live oaks and, in that frame, the picture of waving marsh grass and the mucky channels reaching out to the ocean and the blue sky. Margaret Hall, the wife of Captain Basil Hall, visiting Darien in the late 1820s, had called it "a pretty little town."[17] The spot which had pleased Oglethorpe in the beginning had never lost its natural beauty.

---

[14]Coulter, *Thomas Spalding,* p. 147.

[15]Ibid., pp. 182ff.

[16]The University of Georgia Library has microfilm copies of the *Darien Gazette,* 1818-1828 (incomplete). Originals are owned by Miss Bessie Lewis, Darien, the late Mrs. Craig Barrow, Wormsloe, and the following: The Library of the State of Georgia has a broken file, 1824-Apr. 12, 1825; Yale University Library has July 22, Aug. 12, Sept. 2, 1828; the Library of Congress has July 20, 1824; the American Antiquarian Society has Apr. 25, May 16, June 6, 27, July 11, 25, Aug. 17-24, Sept. 14-Oct. 10, 31-Dec. 5, 1822; May 18, 1824. Emory University Library has a file of *The McIntosh County Herald,* Jan. 22-Oct. 8, 1839; Nov. 12-Dec. 31, 1839; Jan. 7-Jan. 28, Feb. 4, 1840 (incomplete). The Library of Congress has the first issue of the *Darien Phoenix,* Jan. 22, 1829. No issue of the *Darien Telegraph* has been located.

[17]Margaret Hall, *The Aristocratic Journey* . . . (New York and London, 1931), p. 234.

Men in the town and near it built their lumber yards and sawmills, their docks and shipping wharves, and warehouses and stores. Commercial firms in Darien did business with Liverpool. Before 1820 Sawyer and Herring had a general store where one could buy anything from brandy to carriages, and Rufus Merrill's Variety Store advertised in the Darien *Gazette* such items as snuff, sawmills, and silver toothpicks.[18] In time the local paper pointed with pride "to our city as an important Lumber Market," and considered lumber "full of promise to the prosperity of Darien."[19] The people built their schools[20] and their churches, and, of course, their saloons and taverns—the Darien Hotel, the Eagle Hotel, and the Mansion House.

As the rice and cotton planters and the timber merchants began to prosper there were those in other walks of life who were eager to get some of their profits. Among those who took the planters' and merchants' money, and enhanced the cultural atmosphere of the community as well, was an artist by the name of Harding who announced in the *McIntosh Herald* that he had

---

[18]See Coulter, *Thomas Spalding*, 174. An examination of advertisements in early issues of the *Darien Gazette* suggests a healthy economic growth. In addition to Sawyer and Herring's general store and Merrill's Variety Store, some others advertising groceries and drygoods were Dewitt and Burnett, Yonge and Richardson, J. H. Giekie and Co., C. Thayer, Anson Kimberly, B. King and Co., C. M'Gregor and Co., William Turner and Co., and C. G. Jones and Co. John B. Mills carried drygoods and hardware. Hall, Cooke and Co. carried among other things tobacco, rum, and bricks. Bricks could also be bought from Gray and Layman. Boots and shoes could be bought at Davis and Kelly's, Peck and Beardslee's, and Perry Davis and Co. Hart and Co., in one advertisement, featured baby bootees and brandy. Joseph Depass and Co. had a good line of liquors, and Philo Hurd and Co. carried saddles, Courts E. Roughton ran a livery stable. William B. Holzendorf was not only the postmaster but ran a boarding house and a general store as well. Daniel Jackson and Lewis Adams sold books and stationery. J. Maunder sold drugs and medicines, and Nathaniel Cornwell and John White were watchmakers and jewelers. Downer and Eaton were manufacturers making coaches and chairs, and B. and J. English sold furniture. Samuel and David Hamilton leased stores and wharves, and George Street sold real estate. Cotton and lumber could be stored in Thomas Jones's warehouse. Items chosen at random from early issues of the *Darien Gazette*, Nov. 2 (Vol. 1, No. 2), 1818-Mar. 10, 1821.

[19]*The McIntosh County Herald*, Jan. 22, 1839.

[20]In 1819 McIntosh Academy promised its patrons "instructors whose talents, attainments and morals meet the approbation of the commissioners" and assured them that they would give "particular attention . . . to the health, manners and morals of the scholars." On November 6, 1824 a Mrs. Lindon announced the opening of Adelphi Academy for young ladies. *Darien Gazette,* Aug. 9, 1819; Nov. 6, 1824.

taken rooms at the Mansion House where those who might wish to have portraits done could see "specimens of his painting."[21] Music, too, had a place in the life of the town. A traveler coming through by stage from Macon stopped over night at one of the taverns where he was serenaded by young voices outside his window. He was so greatly impressed by the musical talents of the young people that he wrote the editor a letter complimenting them.[22] He left the next day for Savannah, getting up in time to catch the stage scheduled to depart at 4:00 in the morning.[23] Doctors, too, were eager to treat their patients and collect their fees.[24]

A major part of Darien's social life was related to water sports. A boat named, for some unknown reason, the *C.C.S.* was owned by Gignilliat and Stockwell. Although it had only four oars, it beat Captain Floyd's six-oared *Caroline King* in a race at St. Mary's in the Third Annual Regatta of the Aquatic Club of Georgia. But soon after that the *Caroline King* raced Captain Bryan's six-oared *Victoria* in Darien and beat her in a half-mile race. Bets were two-to-one on the *Caroline King* which won by one length in two minutes and forty-five seconds.[25] Further evidence of social life can be seen in the fact that plans for a Masonic hall were being made by the men of the town in 1819. Evidence both of social and cultural interest is seen in an announcement in the Darien *Gazette* in July of that year to the effect that the Reading Room and Bar was open and ready for the use of the gentlemen. [26] There might have been a hint of more social life than culture in such an establishment.

Culture was at low tide in this coastal town, but the economic situation had deteriorated to a point correspondingly low in the 1840s. A serious economic depression hit the Delta and drastically affected the entire agricultural South in that decade. Darien suffered badly and most of its business reflected the depression. The price of cotton dropped to a record low

---

[21] *The McIntosh County Herald*, Feb. 5, 1839.

[22] *Ibid.*, Aug. 20, 1839.

[23] "The Darien Stage will, in the future, start precisely at 4 o'clock in the morning of every Tuesday and Friday, from William B. Holzendorf's boarding house. No responsibility on the proprietor when passengers fail to attend at the hour stated, and no money returned under any circumstances whatever." *Darien Gazette*, May 31, 1819.

[24] Dr. William Fraser begins the practice of "medicine, surgery, etc., in Darien, and tenders his services to its inhabitants and the vicinity." *Darien Gazette*, July 19, 1819.

[25] *The McIntosh County Herald*, Feb. 26, 1839.

[26] *Darien Gazette*, July 19, 1819; July 26, 1819.

and the rice planters were also at the mercy of the commission merchant on the one hand and fickle weather on the other—weather which could, and often did, change overnight, often ruining a $100,000 crop. But by the end of the decade the economy was improving. The 1850s brought prosperity to the South, and Darien began to profit from the rising tide that brought better conditions.

In time Darien was carrying on a thriving timber business. It was the promise of timber and the persuasive arguments of Tom Hilton's grandmother Jane Lachlison Hilton that caused Tom's grandfather to close out his building business in Preston, England and sail the rough seas to Darien where he started his lumber company with a sawmill on Cathead Creek.[27] Tom's Uncle Robert was the first of the Lachlisons to come to Georgia when he installed heavy English-made machinery in a Savannah mill about 1840. Fifteen years later his Uncle James came. Then some of the Hilton boys. And that, as Tom put it, was too much for Gandmother Jane, so she made Grandfather Thomas Hilton close out his business, sell his houses, and make the long journey to Darien.

Tom remembered how his father described lumbering on the Altamaha. The small sailing boats, brigs, or brigantines, carried no more than half the cargo that three-masted schooners of a later day carried in coastwise trade. The cargo was, for the most part, timbers sent to New England for ship building. The crews propelled the little boats up the river to the mill by pushing them with long poles. They came in over Doboy Bar, Darien being about nine miles inland. Settlers living above Darien floated cotton and other farm products down the river on flat boats or rafts. Most of these rafts were dismantled after reaching their destination and the lumber was sold—a profitable system. Fanny Kemble called the rafts Oconee boxes and described such a vessel as being "nothing but a monstrous square box, made of rough planks, put together in the roughest manner."[28]

The timber was mostly long-leaf yellow pine. Farmers along the river cut this fine-grained timber and "squared it with the broad axe, as was the custom in those times," then they dragged the logs, usually with oxen, to the water where they made large rafts of them. The raft hands cooked on the crude vessel and tied it up at night to trees on the bank. At Darien an inspector measured their timber. It was then sold to a mill or to an exporter. The journey back home was very difficult until the railroad came. Tom Hilton recalled how the raft hands got home after the coming of the railroad. They

---

[27]Thomas Hilton, *High Water on the Bar* (Savannah, 1951).

[28]Kemble, 61.

would hire a man to row them across the channels of the Altamaha, "up Hammersmith's Creek on the Glynn County side to a landing." Then they would walk some six or eight miles to "Old Number One," a flag station on the Southern Railroad out of Brunswick. They would usually get off at Jesup or perhaps Everett, or the station nearest their homes, and walk some more. Not having been to a town for months, they would take their timber money and celebrate in one or more of Darien's popular saloons.[29]

In time palatial steamboats began to ply the Altamaha and move up the Oconee to Milledgeville, the state capital, and up the Ocmulgee to Macon, a middle-Georgia cotton city of considerable importance after 1840. Ships began to carry cargo to and from Charleston, Savannah, New York, and foreign ports. Mills hummed upon the high bluff of the river near the location of old Fort King George and at Cathead, and Darien reached a proud and prominent place in the commercial world. The social life began to reflect more and more the prosperity of the town, and culture began to take on greater significance.

But there came a time when Northern politicians and Southern politicians could find no final answer as a compromise between their conflicting interests. Southern states withdrew from the Union and organized a confederacy of their own. Then war broke out between North and South and, suddenly, on a June day in 1863 Darien was burned—not by an Act of God but by lighted pine torches carried in black hands. Burned by black soldiers, yes, but at the command of a white colonel from Kansas assisted by the young, idealistic Colonel Shaw from Boston.

---

[29]Hilton, 4-5.

II

LESSONS IN RETALIATION

Some of the hate that burst into flame at Darien in June, 1863, was kindled years before on the plains of Kansas in the heart of James Montgomery, the Western abolitionist who later would lead South Carolina and Georgia Negroes in sacking and burning Darien. Montgomery was the ranking officer at St. Simons who would take Robert Shaw, the Massachusetts colonel, on the raid which ended in the destruction of that pretty little river town. In Kansas Montgomery was simply a Jayhawker, but on the South Atlantic coast he would be known and feared by the planters as the colonel of the Second South Carolina Volunteers, a Negro regiment whose duty it was to harass the countryside. While Darien was growing into a thriving little shipping town after its economic depression of the 1840's, Montgomery was busily engaged in bloody warfare against slave owners in Kansas and Missouri.

The proslavery people who moved into the Kansas Territory called the Western abolitionists "Jayhawks," or "Jayhawkers," but Mongomery and his neighbors didn't seem to mind the appellation, at least not so long as they could retaliate. And retaliate they did, house for house as Bushwhackers and Jayhawkers played their fearful burning game. "Bushwhackers" was the name by which proslavery Westerners were known. It is said the term "Jayhawker" originated with a raw-boned Irishman named Pat Delvin. Pat returned one day to Kansas after several days in Missouri with his horse packed to capacity with all sorts of things. A crowd gathered around and someone asked how he came upon all that loot which they recognized as utensils which had been stolen from them earlier and were now being brought back. The resourceful Pat replied, "Back home in Ireland there was a jay hawk that just took things, and I suppose my horse has somehow acquired the habit of that bird."[1]

Slave-owning Bushwhackers several years before the destruction of Darien had burned Montgomery out and forced him to crawl about in the grass like a snake to avoid capture and possible death. This Western abolitionist had spent his boyhood days in Kentucky where he was born in 1814, but had moved to Missouri and thence to Kansas Territory in time to get into the thick of the war raging there between Southerners who were trying to organize a slave state and the antislavery group who were determined to make it free.

The Jayhawkers had to be constantly on the alert to avoid sudden attacks by the proslavery Bushwhackers who might ambush them without a moment's notice. The Bushwhackers roamed about, sometimes singly and sometimes in gangs. These Southerners were determined to make Kansas territory theirs and to destroy any who opposed them. Montgomery's farm was five miles west of Mound City which, in turn, was ten miles west of the Missouri line and about twenty miles north of Fort Scott. He was besieged one night as he sat in his home with his wife Clarinda and the children. Bullets zinged across the room at window level from time to time through the night so that father, mother and children had to lie on the floor to avoid being hit. Then early in the year 1855,[2] the proslavery Bushwhackers surrounded Montgomery's house and set fire to it. The occupants were forced to stand and watch their home burn while all their possessions went up in smoke. After this Montgomery began to gather his antislavery neighbors together in secret hiding places and organize a force for resistance. He was a part-time preacher, but his ruthlessness made him appear to be more a ruffian than a man of the cloth. Nevertheless, the role of a cleric made him fight with a zeal and fanaticism akin to that of John Brown, his friend and companion in the territorial war. His wrath was in part a righteous anger, but the lessons in hate made him, finally, a fanatical seeker of vengeance. Long before Robert Shaw was asked to recruit a regiment of Negroes to go South and help free the slaves Montgomery and the Westerners were feeling the anger of slaveowners, learning to hate them, and practicing retaliation against them. When Colonel Shaw set out on his Georgia journey in May, 1863, he was to find already

---

[1]William A. Mitchell, *Linn County, Kansas: A History* (Kansas City, 1928), 22.
[2]*Ibid.,* 17.

there the Western colonel who had learned about retaliation on Kansas plains.

Open war had broken out in the Kansas territory in the spring of 1856. The Jayhawkers had received a shipment of rifles—"Beecher's Bibles"—from the East. News of this angered the Bushwhackers, and they got ready to move against the Jayhawkers. The Bushwhackers were led by an ex-Georgian named George W. Clark. Starting from West Point, Missouri, Clark with five hundred followers covered a path ten miles in width burning the homes of the Jayhawkers, running off their cattle and horses, raping their women, and hauling away all the loot they could carry with them.[3] Typical of their atrocious crimes was the killing of a free-state settler, an old man by the name of Denton who lived on the Osage River. Clark's men called the old man to his door one night and riddled his frail body with buck shot. Their only purpose was "to strike terror into the hearts of the many free-state settlers along the Osage River." Montgomery, too, was among Clark's intended victims. He was hotly pursued by Clark's men, but managed to escape through the brush.[4]

Then the Jayhawkers struck back. Led by the notorious James Henry Lane they marched to the Missouri border shouting, "Everything disloyal . . . must be cleaned out."[5] Border ruffians joined the Kansas proslavery men to retaliate in the attack of Lawrence. Among the approximately eight-hundred Bushwhackers making the attack on Lawrence on May 21 was Colonel Jefferson Buford's company and the "Kickapoo Rangers."[6] They burned down the Free State Hotel, pillaged homes, destroyed the presses of the local papers, and killed two of the citizens.

But the Bushwhackers were soon made to pay for their crimes. John Brown joined Montgomery and his men. He came blood-stained from Pottawatomie Creek where he, with four sons and three other men, had tasted revenge on May 24 in a midnight massacre in which five proslavery settlers were killed near Dutch Henry's Crossing. James Montgomery was very hospitable to John Brown, and Brown found him to be "a man to his liking."[7] Although Montgomery's fort was always open to him, Brown found his gang too numerous for the house that served both as fort and Montgomery's

---

[3]*Ibid.*, p. 20.

[4]*Ibid.*, p. 64.

[5]Albert Castel, *A Frontier State at War* . . . (Ithaca, 1958), p. 53.

[6]Richard B. Morris, ed., *Encyclopedia of American History* (New York, 1953). p. 220.

[7]Mitchell, p. 20.

domicile, so he constructed a fort of his own. Nevertheless, the two men continued to work together in close harmony. Their following increased and both gangs grew steadily larger.

In May, 1858, at Harper's Ferry, the year before John Brown made what turned out to be his last raid, he and Montgomery were taught another lesson in violence that galvanized their hatred of proslavery forces. Charles Hamilton, a Missouri Bushwhacker who was in Kansas with his gang "to kill snakes," as he expressed it, rode to the Trading Post with his outlaws intent on murdering some of the settlers there. The Trading Post was about thirty miles north of Fort Scott on the road that led to Kansas City. It was about five miles north of Mound City and about three miles west of the Missouri line. Between the Trading Post and the Missouri line was a swampy area through which flowed a river running eastward by way of Osceola, Missouri. Early French explorers had named the place "Le Marais du Cygne", and the river which becomes the Osage on the Missouri side is called the Marais des Cygnes in Kansas. Gideon Potts and John Gates organized posses to drive the Bushwhackers back into Missouri. Hamilton's force left the Trading Post ahead of them, taking a number of captives with them as they rode off. Potts and Gates, with what neighbors they could quickly gather, mounted their horses and pursued the ruffians. When they came to the Marais du Cygne they found eleven bodies stiffening in death to give mute testimony of the cruelty of the Missourians.[8] The news of this massacre spread widely throughout the North and stirred angry passion in abolitionist poet Whittier's breast, causing him to pen these lines:

> From the hearths of their cabins,
>   The fields of their corn,
> Unwarned and unweaponed,
>   The victims were torn,—
> By the whirl wind of murder
>   Swooped up and swept on
> To the low, reedy fen-lands,
>   The Marsh of the Swan.[9]

The fire of hate then burned brightly. Montgomery and Brown with the horror of the massacre heavy upon them resolved to carry revenge as far as possible. As it turned out, Brown carried his hate to Virginia and the gallows; Montgomery carried his revenge to Darien. Brown carried revenge to a

---

    [8]*Ibid.*, 42.

    [9]"Le Marais du Cygne" was first published in *The Atlantic Monthly*, vol. II (Sept., 1858), 429.

martyr's grave; Montgomery burned some of his hate out at Darien and then returned to his Kansas home.[10] But Montgomery had yet more fighting to do in the Kansas territory before organizing runaway slaves in South Carolina and meeting Robert Shaw at Darien.

After the fall of Fort Sumter in April, 1861, both Union and Confederate governments were busily engaged in organizing military forces and accepting volunteer companies. Lincoln had proclaimed a state of armed rebellion after the Confederates captured that Federal bastion in Charleston harbor. Four more states then seceded and joined the newly-formed Confederate States of America. One of them, Virginia, became the home state of the Confederacy.

All of the ruthlessness was not practiced merely in the West, nor was all the villainy to be found in the camp of the Yankees. An incident occurred in Virginia which shows a reckless disregard for private property on the part of the Southerners. The Rebels did what the Yankees called a foolish thing, an example, one might say, of anger without reason. They burned the town of Hampton, at the mouth of the James River. Thus Southerners were destroying the homes of their own people. This occurred in August, 1861. General J. Bankhead Magruder was in command of the Confederate forces and, excited over the news of the rout of the Federals at Manassas, he ordered a force of two thousand men into the vicinity of Hampton. As the enemy evacuated the town in great haste, he ordered it to be burned. Captain R.A. Smith of the Macon Volunteers wrote home to his friend J.W. Burke in Macon, Georgia about it. He said, "We distinctly saw the fire and have clearly seen the chimneys left standing since the fire of that once flourishing village."[11] In the opinion of Captain Smith the burning of Hampton was a "military necessity,"[12] and General Magruder explained the reason why Virginia planters had to be burned out by their own army. He said he had known "for some time that Hampton was the harbor of runaway slaves and traitors, and . . . that it could not be held by us even if taken."[13] When he saw the "extreme importance" of the town to the Federals and realized that "the town itself would lend great strength to whatever fortifications they might

---

[10]His biographer says Montgomery returned from the war "pretty much an invalid, and gave the greater part of this time to reading and preaching." Mitchell, 29f.

[11]Capt. R. A. Smith to J. W. Burke. This letter, written from Sewell's Point, Va., Aug. 14, 1861, is in the possession of Mrs. Daly Smith, Macon, Ga.

[12]*Ibid.*

[13]*Official Records of the Union and Confederate Armies in the War of the Rebellion* (Washington, 1880-1901), ser. I. vol. 4, p. 571. Hereafter cited *OR: Armies.*

erect around it" he determined to burn it immediately.[14] He claimed that some Hampton residents themselves, who were evacuated, "seemed to concur" with him as to "the propriety" of his action.[15]

Whatever justification the action might have had in the eyes of Union sympathizers in the South, the Northerners looked upon it as an act of mad vengeance and blind hate and considered the destruction of Southern property by Southerners as a foolish passion. Magruder argued, however, that he was striking a blow at "traitors" and trying to destroy a colony of freed slaves as well as to gain a strategic advantage over the enemy. Union general Benjamin F. Butler, later of "Beast Butler" fame at New Orleans, wrote to General Winfield Scott from Fortress Monroe the day after the burning of Hampton saying, ". . . in a single hour the rebel army devoted to indiscriminate destruction both public and private buildings, the church and the court-house. . . . This act upon the part of the enemy seems to me to be a representative one, showing the spirit in which the war is to be carried on on their part, and which perhaps will have a tendency to provoke a corresponding spirit upon our part."[16]

Civil war having spread from the plains of Kansas to its wider stage, Montgomery would no longer lead his Jayhawkers in lawless retaliation against Bushwhackers, but would now command a regiment of the United States Army and conduct his raids in legalized warfare and spill blood legitimately. No longer in his ragged and grotesque uniform would he lead a hodgepodge of Kansas Jayhawkers, for the Secretary of War had accepted into the Army of the United States his Third Kansas Regiment, consisting of two companies of cavalry and two of artillery.[17] On June 20, 1861, Montgomery was placed in charge of the post at Fort Scott under the command of the ruffian James H. Lane, then a brigadier general, with headquarters at Fort Leavenworth.[18] On September 3, Colonel Montgomery and his fellow officers "behaved admirably," according to the fiery Lane, in a two-hour encounter with the Confederates just twelve miles east of Fort Scott;[19] but Confederate General Sterling Price, commanding the Missouri

---

[14] *Ibid.*

[15] *Ibid.*

[16] *Ibid.*, 568. Gen. Butler was the first to experiment in confiscating slaves as contraband of war.

[17] *OR: Armies,* ser. III, vol. 1, p. 282.

[18] *Ibid.*, ser. IV, vol. 3, p. 453.

[19] *Ibid.*, 163.

State Guard, forced Montgomery to abandon that fort on the twenty-first.[20] This was a familiar experience for the Kansas colonel who had been driven out of his own home-fort many times by proslavery Bushwhackers back in the days when war was simply retaliation between lawless gangs.

Lane and Montgomery then burned Osceola, a Missouri town on the Osage about fifty miles east of Fort Scott. Fifteen Southerners were killed. Lane's report boasted that they had burned that town "to ashes."[21] The word spread widely that they were "destroying the property of Southern men."[22] General Sterling Price complained to General McCulloch that Lane, Montgomery and others, supported by the United States forces, "are not only desolating the country, but are committing the most barbarous outrages upon the people of that region."[23]

The spirit of revenge was high on both sides in 1861. Southerners had burned churches in Virginia and destroyed the property of their own people, claiming them to have been "traitors," and Western abolitionists had burned towns belonging to the proslavery people in the Trans-Mississippi region in retaliation for the suffering they had been forced to endure.

Montgomery, after another year of practicing incendiary acts in Kansas and learning well the technique of plunder and pillage, would then be ordered to the coast of South Carolina to raise a regiment of black troops. Contraband Negroes and runaway slaves from the South Atlantic coastal plantations were to be mobilized as the Second South Carolina Volunteers.[24] The Western Jayhawker would receive his orders the middle of January, 1863. But while he was learning his lessons in retaliation on the plains of Kansas, a Union fleet was preparing to move to South Atlantic waters. All this was prologue to the tragedy at Darien where the flame of hate was to blaze at its greatest intensity in the summer of 1863.

---

[20]*Ibid.*, 185.

[21]Lane to Fremont, Sept. 24, 1861, *OR: Armies,* ser. I, vol. 3, p. 196.

[22]Letter from Brig. Gen. Benjamin McCulloch, Camp Jackson, Ark., Sept. 25, 1861, to Col. T. C. Hindman, Fayetteville, Ark. *Ibid.,* vol. 53, p. 743.

[23]Price to McCulloch, Dec 6, 1861. *Ibid.,* vol. 8, p. 702.

[24]*OR: Armies,* ser. III, vol, 3, p. 14.

III

HILTON HEAD

In THE fall of 1861 Captain Samuel F. Du Pont's South Atlantic Blockading Squadron left Hampton Roads, Virginia for an unidentified port. The ship's captains were to break their sealed orders only after reaching the open sea. The *Wabash*, Du Pont's flagship, led the Union fleet of fifty ships carrying thirteen thousand soldiers through Chesapeake Bay on October 29.[1] The troops were under the command of General Thomas W. Sherman, not to be confused with the red-headed general who marched through Georgia and the Carolinas four years later. The squadron's objective was to effectuate the blockade of South Atlantic ports in accordance with Lincoln's proclamation of April 19. In order to make the President's proclamation a reality, not only would a base of operations have to be secured but as much destruction of property as possible should be accomplished all along the coastal region. The life of the rich tidewater planters should be disrupted, the slaves set free and, if possible, made soldiers to fight for their own freedom. General Sherman's large landing force would be used in taking and holding the territory in that area.

The fleet had embarked at Annapolis on October 21 and reached Hampton Roads the next day, but was unable to set out for Southern waters

---

[1] *Official Records of the Union and Confederate Navies in the War of the Rebellion* (Washington, 1894-1972), ser. I. vol. 12, pp. 230ff. Hereafter cited *OR: Navies.* Captain Du Pont rose to the rank of vice-admiral.

until the twenty-ninth because of bad weather. When the sealed orders were opened the captains learned their destination was Port Royal Sound, South Carolina, the deepest natural harbor on the South Atlantic coast. When the Union Armada reached the waters off the North Carolina shore at Cape Hatteras the fury of the winds scattered the ships. The major portion of the fleet arrived at Port Royal on November 4. At least two transport steamers had been lost at sea and two others did not arrive in time for the battle which was fought on November 7. The large landing force under General Sherman was virtually intact, however, and ready and eager to capture the two forts guarding the entrance to the Sound, Fort Walker on the northeast corner of Hilton Head Island and Fort Beauregard at Bay Point on Phillips Island which was about three miles away protecting the Sound from the North side.

By mid-afternoon on the fourth, thirty-two Union war steamers and transports had collected just off the Sound. Brigadier General Thomas Fenwick Drayton, Confederate commander of that district, left his headquarters at Beaufort, sailing past the enemy fleet to appraise the situation. Thomas Drayton was of an old and honored South Carolina family. One of the federal officers, Captain Percival Drayton of the sloop *Pocahontas*, was his own brother who had renounced his native state at the outbreak of war.[2] General Drayton observed Commodore Josiah Tattnall's little Confederate fleet standing by and saw the Commodore viewing the Union fleet through his long brass spyglass. Tattnall's fleet consisted of a frail river steamboat, the *Savannah,* carrying one 32-pounder smooth-bore gun as its only armament and three tugs improvised into men-of-war, the *Sampson* and *Resolute*, wooden side-wheelers, and the *Lady Davis*, an iron-plated steamer. The three converted tugs mounted one gun each.[3] Obviously, the Confederate boats were no match for the powerful South Atlantic Squadron which included fifteen warships carrying a total of 155 guns ranging up to eleven-inch cannon.

For two days Flag Officer Tattnall's tugs posing as gunboats defied the Union fleet. They were securely hidden in Scull Creek flowing into Port Royal Sound from the southwest and meeting the waters of Beaufort River flowing in from the northwest. On the morning of the fifth the Confederate vessels led by the paddle wheel *Savannah* sailed out defiantly and threw a few shells at

---

[2]For an account of the Drayton family's divided loyalties see Robert Carse, *Department of the South; Hilton Head Island in the Civil War* (Columbia S. C., The State Printing Co., 1961), Appendix A.

[3]*The Savannah Republican,* Nov. 12, 1861 as quoted in *OR: Navies,* ser. I, vol. 12, p. 295.

the Union fleet standing off at the entrance to the Sound. It was only a harmless gesture of boldness, however, and when answered by the Federals they drew back into Scull Creek again out of reach. Tattnall repeated this bold act the next morning with the same poor results.

Regardless of the weakness of Commodore Tattnall's little fleet, Flag Officer Du Pont feared the Confederate forces were too strong for General Sherman to make a successful landing on Hilton Head, his first objective. Debarkation would have to be made five or six miles from Fort Walker. This fort was the stronger of the two Port Royal batteries. The Union fleet had lost some of its equipment to be used for disembarking. Therefore, it was decided to reduce the forts by a raking fire from the fifteen warships rather than risk a landing.

Fort Walker was commanded by Colonel William C. Heyward and defended by 622 men. There were twenty guns of various caliber mounted upon the ramparts. Thirteen guns were on the channel battery, including some rifled cannon. General Drayton on inspecting the fort the day before the battle had found it defended by two companies of Colonel Wagner's First Artillery, South Carolina Militia, three companies of Colonel Heyward's ninth Regiment, South Carolina Volunteers, and four companies of Colonel R. G. M. Dunovant's Twelfth Regiment, South Carolina Volunteers, under Major Cadwalader Jones.[4] In the afternoon about five hunderd reinforcements arrived from Savannah bringing with them two 12-pound Howitzers.

At nine-twenty-five on the morning of the seventh a 9-inch Dahlgren at Fort Walker belched fire toward the 48-gun *Wabash* which was leading the fifteen warships in an elliptical movement toward Hilton Head. But the shell exploded near the muzzle and fell harmlessly. Guns from both forts now fired with increasing rapidity. Heavy firing continued on land and water. The Union fleet sailed by Fort Walker, apparently unharmed. Then, knifing through the waves, the ships circled and fired at Fort Beauregard and repeated the elliptical movement again and again causing more and more damage to both forts.

The Confederates fought bravely for four and a half hours. But by two o'clock in the afternoon, with all but three of Fort Walker's guns on the Hilton Head water front silenced and with little powder left in the magazine, the Confederates abandoned the demolished fort. Reports of the Confederate officers all tell of the bravery of the defenders. Colonel Wagner's fifteen-year-old son, Private Julius Wagner, had leaped upon the rampart to raise

---

[4]*Ibid.,* p. 301.

the fallen Palmetto banner.[5] Such was the stubborn but ineffective resistance of the defenders of Hilton Head.

The defenders of Phillips Island numbered 640 men, commanded by Colonel R. G. M. Dunovant of the Twelfth Regiment, South Carolina Volunteers. Captain Stephen Elliott, son of Georgia's Episcopal bishop, was in immediate command of the 149 troops of the Beaufort Volunteer Artillery which garrisoned Fort Beauregard at Bay Point. The remainder were troops of Colonel Dunovant's regiment defending the eastern part of the island. General Thomas Sherman sent three brigades to take possession of Fort Walker and at dawn the next morning the New York Highland Guard, a detachment of one of the brigades, boarded a gunboat and took possession of what was left of Fort Beauregard.

When the fighting ended and the casualty count was made it was found that of the Confederates killed, ten of them had been slain inside Fort Walker. Twenty were wounded inside that fort and thirteen were wounded inside Fort Beauregard. Only eight Federals had been killed.[6] Du Pont waded ashore at Hilton Head Island to participate in a burial service honoring the eight Union soldiers who had died in the battle. After the volleys had been fired and the graves filled and marked the burial party quickly returned to camp, for there was much work to do in getting the Union headquarters ready for a base of operations.

The Federals, after their comparatively easy capture of the forts guarding the deep harbor at Port Royal, were fully confident that they could move on to the conquest of the whole area and perhaps bring about the fall of Charleston, about fifty miles to the north of Hilton Head, and Savannah, about forty miles south of the newly acquired base of operation. But General Robert E. Lee, who had been transferred from the mountains of western Virginia to the South Atlantic coast to strengthen the defenses, had done well the work of improving the batteries at both places. The Federals did get a foothold on Tybee Island off Savannah and from that point had gone on to capture Fort Pulaski on Cockspur Island on April 10, 1862, but the coastal cities proved to be more difficult than the Federals expected them to be. Union officers began to quarrel with one another when their hope of conquering the whole region grew dim and faded. Although Fort Pulaski fell in the spring of 1862 and Fort Wagner, the bastion on Morris Island at Charleston, was to surrender in the fall of the next year Savannah and Charleston remained in Confederate hands until the end of the war. The rail

---

[5]See Col. Wagener's Report, *ibid.,* 308.

[6]See Gen. Drayton's Report, *ibid.,* 306.

link between these cities also remained unbroken. Nevertheless, the Federals harassed the region from South Carolina to Florida. Operating from Hilton Head they raided the towns and plantations up and down the coast. The name of the Hilton Head fort was changed to Fort Welles in honor of Gideon Welles, Secretary of the Navy. Then General Sherman went to work rebuilding and improving it. As it turned out, he was a more successful builder than a field commander, but he remained in command at Hilton Head until late in the spring of 1862.

On May 9, General David Hunter succeeded Sherman as commander of the Southern Department which consisted of South Carolina, Georgia, and Florida. Hunter, who had driven Major General Sterling Price's army back to St. Louis in the Missouri campaign the previous November, was a barrel-chested man with rounded shoulders. He wore a long drooping mustache that curved downward framing a prominent chin which rested on a thick neck. His dark hair almost covered his ears but sat on his receding forehead like a wig that had slipped backwards. His dark and piercing eyes, deep-set under heavy eyebrows, were widely separated by a well-shaped Roman nose.

Much of the work of harassment, as General Hunter planned it, was to be done by Negroes; and he began immediately to build up an army of ex-slaves and "contrabands," as he called the captured Negroes. In order to build up a black army, Hunter proclaimed freedom for all slaves in the Southern Department. On the very day that he took command at Hilton Head, he bristled as best he could his drooping mustache and dictated to an aide: "Slavery and martial law in a free country are altogether incompatible. The persons in these three states, Georgia, Florida, and South Carolina, heretofore held as slaves are therefore declared forever free."[7] He had already decided what to do with the freed Negroes, the runaway slaves, and even the reluctant Negroes who might wish to stay in the fields rather than obey as soldiers the orders of Yankee officers. He wrote General Isaac Stevens who was commanding Port Royal Island at Beaufort saying he was authorized by the War Department "to form negroes into 'squads, companies, or otherwise' as I deem most beneficial to the public service."[8] He went on to say that he planned to recruit two regiments of them to be led by white officers.

May 9 was a busy day for Hunter. He had lost no time in issuing his emancipation proclamation. Another order coming from the new commander's headquarters that day was directed to the officers of the northern and southern districts of the Southern Department. They were to

---

[7] *The New York Herald,* May 16, 1862.

[8] *Ibid.,* 30.

send immediately "to those headquarters, under guard, all the able-bodied negroes capable of bearing arms ..."9 The first company was to come from Beaufort. General Stevens from his quarters in the stately Weymouth house in Beaufort issued a circular on Sunday, May 11, declaring that "the agents and overseers of the plantations must send to Beaufort [the next morning] every able-bodied negro between the ages of fifteen and forty-five years capable of bearing arms."10

Such a sweeping order was disapproved by federal officials in Washington, by the President himself, and even by some of the Abolitionists. Edward Pierce, Special Agent of the Treasury Department who also lived for a time in the magnificent two-story white-columned Weymouth house facing the bay in Beaufort, looked upon Monday the twelfth of May as "a sad day" indeed. He said the slaves were "taken from the fields [and] the soldiers, under orders ... loaded their guns, so that the negroes might see what would take place in case they attempted to get away ..."11 On some plantations "the wailing and screaming were loud and the women threw themselves in dispair on the ground." Some Negroes "took to the woods and were hunted up by the soldiers."12 Pierce, being in charge of Union-controlled plantations producing foodstuff and material for the Federals, would rather have the Negroes work the fields than serve as soldiers. Laura Towne, one of the many Northern teachers who came South to help educate Negroes uprooted by the war, called it "the black day." She was of the opinion that General Hunter's order was a "tyranny" that caused "dismay and indignation." She thought it a "rash" decision to take Negroes from the fields where they were so well adapted and so badly needed.13 They were content there, she thought, if only they could be free and learn to read and write and be permitted to stay with their families. She was probably right, for few of the Negroes cared for the business of killing and being killed.

9*Ibid.*, 31.

10*Ibid.*, 50. The Weymouth house is now the residence of Mr. and Mrs. Angus Fordham.

11*Ibid.*, 31.

12*Ibid.*, 57.

13Laura M. Towne, *Letters and Diary of Laura M. Towne . . . 1862-1884.* Edited by Rupert Sargent Holland (Cambridge, 1912), 45-47. Miss Towne, a native of Pennsylvania, came to St. Helena Island, S. C., in 1862 and stayed through the Reconstruction period. The Penn School was the result of her efforts in behalf of the Negroes.

The "Hunter Regiment," as it was called, was disbanded on August 11 on orders from The War Department.[14] Those black soldiers had been paid nothing for their services, and during their several months' military duty in the regiment their families had suffered. Hunter, like Fremont in Missouri, was, in the opinion of President Lincoln, moving too fast in emancipating slaves and making soldiers of them. Lincoln had not at the time consented to the abolitionists' demands to take Rebel property under the name of contraband, and he repudiated Hunter's order declaring it "unauthorized and of no validity or effect." He reserved to himself the right to determine whether he could constitutionally "adopt such a policy if the war eventually should make it necessary."[15] Soon after Hunter's regiment was ordered to disband he was given a leave of absence. During his absence the Southern Department was under the command of General Ormsby M. Mitchel. But General Mitchel died on October 30 and Hunter was back again at his command, continuing as commander of the Department until succeeded by General Quincy Gillmore following the burning of Darien in June the next year.[16]

The abolitionists were persistent and kept after the President to adopt the policy of using Negroes in military service. By mid-fall of 1862 the President had changed his position and agreed to permit the enlistment of Southern Negroes to fight under white officers for their own freedom. On October 10 General Rufus Saxton, military governor of the Department of the South, was ordered to raise five thousand Negro troops in that region. Thomas Wentworth Higginson, a captain in the Massachusetts Fifty-Seventh Volunteers doing picket duty near Beaufort, was chosen to be the colonel of the First South Carolina Volunteers.[17] General Saxton offered him the command of the first regiment and Higginson gladly accepted. He knew it would not be easy to train and discipline the ex-slaves unaccustomed to anything but cultivating the fields, but his abolitionist sentiments were strong enough to persuade him to take command. He said, "I had been an abolitionist too long and had known and loved John Brown too well, not to feel a thrill of joy at last on finding myself in the position where he only wished to be."[18] The New England poet, minister and soldier threw himself into the drills on Hilton Head Island with the confidence that he was training the

---

[14]Saxton to Stanton, Oct. 29, 1862. *OR: Armies,* ser. III, vol. 2, p. 695.

[15]*OR: Armies,* ser. III, vol. 2. pp. 42-43. See also *The New York Times.,* May 20, 1862.

[16]*OR: Armies,* ser. I, vol. 14, pp. 376, 380, 388, 464.;

[17]*Ibid.,* ser. III, vol. 4, p. 1027.

[18]Higginson, a graduate of Harvard Divinity School, was intensely Abolitionist in

former slaves to help their black brothers travel the road to freedom. In time the Negroes were performing fairly well their role of liberators.

Captain Charles T. Trowbridge, who would command Company A of Higginson's regiment when mustered in, had done pioneering work in recruiting ex-slaves for military service. It had started back in May when as a sergeant in the New York Volunteer Engineers he had been detailed to raise the so-called "Hunter Regiment." He had taken his Negroes to St. Simons Island on August 5 and taught them to chase their former masters from their homes. On arriving he had found twenty-five Negroes on the island already armed and led by one of their own race who called himself John Brown. In a skirmish with the planters—perhaps the first armed encounter between whites and their former slaves—Brown had been killed. Soon after that, Hunter's Negro regiment had been ordered to disband. That didn't stop Captain Trowbridge. He continued to drill the black people, numbering nearly 200 men, women, and children, outfitted in every conceivable garb. He kept up the farcical drills until October 19 when enlistment of the First South Carolina began and his company became the first in the newly formed regiment.[19]

On November 7 Captain Trowbridge's company of the First South Carolina Volunteers was used in a raid up the Sapelo River. General Saxton, in his report to Secretary Stanton, said he had two objectives in ordering this expedition. The first, to prove that the Negroes would fight, might have been necessary from the Yankee point of view, since "some ... doubted" that they would stand and fight under fire. The second might also have seemed a necessary objective in the Northern mind, but that would be vigorously denied by the citizens of Darien and those who lived along the banks of the Altamaha and the Sapelo and, indeed, all the coastal planters whom the Federals visited during the first week of November, 1862. The way General

---

sentiment. Though he had many relatives in Virginia, it was reported that he had been in closer touch with and was more sympathetic with John Brown than with his Virginia kin. He had entered the ministry as pastor of the Free Church in Worchester. It is said he "preached himself out" of both of these churches as he caught fire for abolitionism. See Katherine M. Jones, *Port Royal Under Six Flags* (Indianapolis, 1960), 262. "The First Regiment of South Carolina Volunteers was mustered into service of the United States in October, 1862, and placed under the command of Col. T. W. Higginson, an able and accomplished officer." Saxton to Stanton, Dec. 30, 1864, in *OR: Armies,* ser. III, vol. 4, p. 1027. See Higginson's own story in *Army Life in a Black Regiment* (Boston, 1870).

[19]Higginson, Appendix B, pp. 272-77.

Saxton expressed it was, "to bring away the people [Negroes] from the mainland, destroy all rebel salt-works, and to break up the rebel picket stations along the line of the coast."[20] Trowbridge's Negroes, numbering sixty-two, were transported on the steamer _Darlington_, a side-wheeler. The raid was led by Colonel Oliver T. Beard of the Forty-Eighth New York Volunteers.[21] The soldiers, white and colored side by side, spread terror from the Sapelo to the Altamaha and alarmed the citizens of McIntosh County from one end of the county to the other. The terror really began on the third when they started out from Florida. They moved up the Georgia coast the next day and at King's Bay were attacked by a force of eighty, of whom they killed two. On the sixth they landed on Butler's Island where they took eighty bushels of rice. They captured three prisoners at Darien. On the seventh, accompanied by the gunboat _Potomska_, Lieutenant William Budd commanding, they went up to the Sapelo. The _Potomska, a screw steamer_, carried five guns. Lieutenant Budd went aboard the _Darlington_ and the raiders then proceeded up the river as far as Fairhope. At Spalding's they were attacked by about eighty defenders. Colonel Beard claimed that his men killed two of them. On the way back down the river as they passed Spalding's they were attacked again. This gave them the excuse to land and burn all the buildings on the place. The _Potomska_ aided the landing party by shelling the woods from a bend in the river.[22] Reuben King's daughter, Sarah Amanda, who had married James Walker in 1839 and had three sons in Confederate service, described the fright she experienced when the expedition reached "Mallow," the King plantation at Pine Harbor sixteen miles from Darien. She wanted her soldier sons to know "exactly what took place the day the abolition thieves" came, so she wrote it all down while it was fresh in her memory:

> We were at the breakfast table, Joe, Isa, my father and myself, my poor mother being too feeble to join us, when the cry of "Yankee vessels!" took us to the front piazza. There was a large vessel and gun boat just in front of the house, between Sutherland's Bluff and Creighton Island. The tide was high, the morning bright and lovely. The scene was altogether beautiful, and the vessels so novel a sight at Mallow that I was constrained in spite of myself to stop and admire the hugh monsters, walking the waters like things of life.

---

[20]_OR: Armies,_ ser. I, vol. 14, p. 189.

[21]Lt. Col. O. T. Beard's report, Nov. 10, 1862, _OR: Armies,_ ser. I, vol. 14, pp. 191, 192.

[22]_Ibid._

When they got to Belleville they sent up a rowboat with a few negroes, who soon returned without firing a single gun. They then proceeded to Mallow at a rapid rate.

I came into the house and sought my father to ask him what I had better to do. He begged that I would keep perfectly composed and remain quietly in the house. We sent Joe [her youngest child, ten years of age] to Fairhope to warn Mr. Dan MacDonald who was at the home and could not see the vessels as they came up. My father thought his gray hairs and my mother's illness would be a protection to us. While we were still speaking, to our surprise a white captain with a drawn sword in his hand followed by a band of negroes marched into the house and stood before us. They had been sent ahead in a row boat. The captain said, "Sir, I have come to demand your Negroes. If you do not give them up there will be great difficulty." My father said nothing. After a few moments silence I said, "Sir, if they are unwilling to go you will not compel them?" He replied, *"Willing or not, they go!"* and turning to the band of black Yankees, gave them orders to shoot down anyone who resisted. Just at this time, Tony came into the yard and two of Mrs. Spalding's men with him. They were instantly seized and secured without the slightest regard for their entreaties and distress. Some of the poor creatures tried to get to us for protection, but were forced away at the point of the bayonet.

The men from the gun boat and vessel now landed. I should say nearly one hundred men came up, most of them Negroes, all armed. Among them was a man differing from the rest in appearance, who had truly taken the "livery of the court of Heaven to serve the devil." He walked in with a number of men and gave us a short but impudent lecture on slavery, and turning to the Negroes said, "We have come to clothe, to educate, to free these poor people, to teach them the Bible and prepare them for heaven." Before he began his speech he enquired of my father his name, which he gave. Then looking at me, he said, "And who are you, woman?" "I am altogether a Southerner, sir," I replied. He said, "I am altogether a Northerner, thank God. The skirt of my garment will never be stained with the blood of slaves." This was the beginning of his lecture. When he concluded my father asked, "Will you be kind enough, sir, to give me your name?" He refused and walked out of the house to welcome his black brethren.

Most of the men now left the house. One whose appearance was very much in favor came up to me and said, "Good morning,

Ma'am. I am captain of the blockading vessel that has been opposite your place for months. I have nothing to do with the slave question and would not have a negro on my vessel if I could help it. I feel very much for the South in this particular, and am sorry enough that things have come to this pass." I felt that this speech in our helpless state was a gift of God. I said, "Sir, if your feelings are with the South, if you do indeed sympathise with her in troubles, I place myself under your protection." At this he bowed politely and said, "If they commence shelling your place, I would advise you to leave the house. Houses stand no chance. If they see a picket, they will certainly shell. Are you acquainted with Captain Brailsford? He has been the cause of this by going on St. Catherine's seizing and killing those Negroes. Since that time we have had orders to leave nothing undone on the coast." I replied, "The Negroes were found in arms against white men, and Captain Brailsford could not have done otherwise." He said, "You are mistaken; they were not found in arms against white men." I said no more. A Yankeeish looking little man said, "The striking of the first blow at Sumter by the South has been the cause of the whole of it." At first I thought I would take no notice of him, but as he looked me full in the face I said, "Striking the first blow at Sumter could not have been avoided. Our personal rights were interfered with. If we carried servants north they were enticed away from us. There was no pleasure in any connection with such people."

Just at this time a band of Negroes and white men came into the yard. I exclaimed, "Gracious heavens! Have I lived to see the day when white men and black are fighting hand to hand on our own soil?" They looked as though they felt the remark. A very genteel man who told me afterward he was an officer in the navy said, "I assure you, Ma'am, it was done first against the North by the South." I said, "I never saw any account of that, nor ever heard of it till today." The men, white and black, were walking about in every direction. My father and I stood on the piazza perfectly unconscious of the scene before us till we heard one of the men remark that Major Bacon, a very old man, had been taken prisoner in Darien. Some of the white men halted by the steps and spoke in a low voice. I heard the word prisoner—the men advanced and the captain with the flaming sword stood in front of us. The idea for the first time flashed into my mind that they were going to seize my father! I clung to him. I pleaded for him. I wept. I know not what I said and did! [Reuben King was at that time in his eighty-fifth year.] The Almighty saved him from the inhuman creatures who would not relieve me by saying they would not take him, but gradually dispersed and went off seeking what they might devour.

They had by this time taken every Negro on the place down to the boat, with the exception of old Ma'am Rose whom they left at the Negroes' houses to die alone. They took off the large copper boilers, a quantity of leather, and everything they wished—helped themselves to oranges and sugar-cane which they carried away in bags. Then they broke into the barn. The famous Captain rushed again into the house and coming up to me said, "Those provisions I find I have orders to either take them or destroy them." I made an exclamation, and said, "You have robbed us of every Negro, and now you are going to make us beggars on the face of the earth." I felt desperate. I knew that our only hope was from the Almighty, and called on Him to deliver us from our enemies. The captain said no more, but walked to the door and stood there for a few minutes.

He then saw some one coming up the avenue on horseback. He immediately gave orders to the band of Negroes who stood near the steps to shoot down anyone who approached. I was in utter despair, knowing that my precious child Joseph had gone over to Mr. MacDonald's, and would now be returning. I knew not where to look or what to say. I begged. I pleaded. I was frantic. I thought I would go to the relief of my child. When I got to the barnyard I discovered about twenty Negroes lying in the grass headed by a white man who stood behind a tree just inside the gate. Joe soon came up. The white man, who, I think, was Irish, said to me, "Is that the boy you have been making all this fuss about? Do you think we would kill such a boy as that?" I replied, "I cannot tell what you would do." "Well, we would not shoot such a boy as that unless he was found with arms, and he would have no business with them." Joe and I walked back to the house as fast as we could, and were indeed thankful to see them all on their way to the vessels.

As they were leaving one of the officers walked back to the house, came in and said to me, "You have had my heartfelt sympathy this day. I have felt very deeply for the family, but could do nothing." He added, "Your father asked the name of the man who spoke to the negroes; he refused to give, but I will. His name is French, the missionary on St. Simons Island whose accounts you may have read." Then taking his leave he hastened to the boats.

During this time my poor mother kept her room being too feeble to take much interest in anything. Isa, dear child, sat by her side, half dead with fright and excitement. My father treated the mixed gang with silent contempt. He said nothing to any of them. I was by his side most of the time.

The blockading vessel stayed at our landing while the gunboat went up to Fairhope where they stole things from the house, broke up the salt works and took Mr. MacDonald prisoner by a band of Negroes. On going up and returning they were fired on with much spirit by the McIntosh cavalry. They in return threw shot and shell thick and fast, but not a single man on our side was hurt. I expected they would stop at Mallow and shell us out, but both the vessel and the gunboat went on to Col. Hopkins' place at Belleville, which they utterly destroyed. Then they went to Capt. Brailsford's, shelled there for about an hour, burned the outbuildings and set fine dwellings on fire, which was extinguished. All this we could see perfectly from Mallow. Night coming on ended their work of destruction for one day.

The inhuman creatures will make my poor old parents suffer. They have not a single servant capable of serving them. They took from us fifty-two Negroes. The few accidentally left are good for very little. My father thinks this place now the safest on the coast. The thieves having been here will not return. I trust he may not be mistaken. God, I trust will be with us—this is all I can hope. I have not now even a little in store for my poor children, but if the Almighty will only return my three soldier sons to me safe and sound when the war is over, I will feel that He has dealt gently with me.

The Negroes were dressed in uniform, red flannel pants and blue coats, with black hats. The captain was dressed handsomely in a new suit of blue-gray with eagle buttons, a very little gold lace, a soft high black hat with gilt designs on the crown, white gloves and his flaming sword.

This is a full account of the whole matter. I may have omitted some things that would interest you, but if we live to meet together again you shall have it from the lips of your dear mother.[23]

---

[23]This eye-witness account of the raid at "Mallow" (Reuben King's plantation) during the Sapelo River raids was published by Sarah Amanda King Walker's daughter, Elizabeth Walker Quarterman, in a little booklet under the title, *The Home*

Saxton was jubilant over the results of the November raids, which he declared were "a perfect success." "Rarely in the progress of this war," he wrote, "has so much mischief been done by so small a force in so short a space of time." He boasted that thirteen different landings had been made. "The pickets in every case were driven in, the salt-works destroyed, and all the work finished up before the enemy could collect a sufficient force to overpower our men."[24] Colonel Beard did a bit of boasting also. He said he started out from St. Simons "with 62 colored fighting men and returned to Beaufort with 156 fighting men (all colored) . . . we brought off 61 women and children. We destroyed nine large salt works, together with $20,000 worth of horses, salt, corn, rice, etc. which we could not carry away."[25]

By the time the Sapelo River raids took place recruiting for the First South Carolina Volunteers was well under way. The first company was mustered in on the very day of the raid at Mallow. Colonel Higginson was commissioned on November 10 and took command of the regiment on the twenty-fourth. The regiment by that time consisted of 500 Negroes.

Meanwhile, Union troops at the Hilton Head base were settling down for a short winter's lull. Colonel Charles G. Halpine, the poet of the Forty-Seventy New York, spent his leisure hours toasting his toes before a wood fire and writing his thoughts in rhyme. Writing under the pen-name of Private Miles O'Reilly, he gave free rein to his crude humor. One poem in particular, called "The Lighter Side," could hardly have been expected to get a laugh from the Negroes. This stanza from the poem is enough to show why:

> Some tell us 'tis a burnin' shame
> To make the naygers fight;
> And that the thrade of bein' kilt
> Belongs but to the white:

---

on the Bluff (n.d., 79 pp.). The original MS is not extant but a typed copy is deposited in the Georgia Historical Society Collection, Savannah, Ga. The expedition up the Sapelo was under the command of Lt. Col. O. T. Beard of the 48th N. Y. Vols. Lt. William Budd commanded the gunboat *Potomska* which proceeded up the Sapelo. According to the log of the *Potomska* they anchored off the King plantation at 10:40 A.M. Lt. Budd, in his report, spoke highly of the Negro soldiers. He said: "They behaved spendidly under the warm and galling fire we were exposed to in two skirmishes with the enemy." The missionary identified as Mr. French was Mansfield French. *OR: Armies*, ser. I. vol. 14, pp. 189-94; *OR: Navies*, ser. I, vol. 13, pp. 438-39. See pictures in *Frank Leslie's Illustrated Weekly*, Dec. 20, 1862, p. 200.

[24]*OR: Armies*, ser. I, vol. 14, p. 190.

[25]*OR: Armies*, ser. I, vol. 14, pp. 191-92; *OR: Navies*, ser. I, vol. 13, pp. 438-39.

But as for me, upon my sowl!
So liberal are we here,
I'll let Sambo be murthered instead of myself,
On every day of the year.
On every day of the year, boys,
And in every hour of the day;
The right to be kilt I'll divide wid him,
And divil a word I'll say.[26]

---

[26]The entire poem, along with other poems and miscellany, is in Halpine's little book, *The Life and Adventures, Songs, Services, and Speeches of Private Miles O'Reilly* (New York, 1864). The poem appears on pages 55-56.

IV

THE SPREAD OF FREEDOM FEVER

As THE year 1863 dawned, Union officers of the Southern Department became more active in executing orders from Saxton's headquarters at Beaufort and Hunter's at Hilton Head. Hunter's headquarters, adjacent to Fort Welles, was a crude one-story building constructed with native pine timber, rough cut. The building faced the ocean. Hunter could see through the frosty window the gray-white sandy beach sloping down to the white-capped waves breaking upon the white sand and turning it gray. "Probably a pretty sight in summer," mused the Union General. But the island was wet and cold and Hunter was in no mood for admiring the wonders of nature. Then came spring and Hunter found even then much discomfort and more as summer drew near: wind blowing hot sand in his face, pesky gnats, sandflies and filthy house flies, and lazy "niggers" lolling around. In General Hunter's calculated judgment Hilton Head was "a helluva place to have a gentlemen's war."

The raids began to embrace more territory. Officers were to disrupt the lives of the planters along the entire coast from Charleston southward well into Florida. Colonel Higginson already had his regiment of Negroes. Now it was up to Colonel Montgomery to recruit another Negro regiment for forays against the towns and countryside. Colonel Robert Shaw would soon begin to recruit Northern Negroes for the Fifty-Fourth Massachusetts and train them at Boston for whatever assignment they might be given on Southern shores. In the meantime, Colonel Montgomery was busy in that kind of work in South Carolina, filling the ranks of the Second South Carolina Volunteers with "contrabands" and runaway slaves. Neither Shaw nor Montgomery would be able to see clearly what his specific orders would be, but General Hunter from his Hilton Head base would direct their movements in due course.

Of the two colonels, Montgomery's job of raising a well disciplined regiment of captured South Carolina and Georgia Negroes and runaway slaves was greater than Shaw's task of raising Northern colored troops. Although Shaw's recruiters would have to seek volunteers beyond the bounds of Massachusetts, they would all be volunteers, willing, some even anxious, to spread freedom fever among the slave population. In the South it was different. A New York *Herald* reporter wrote from Port Royal: "The enlisting of negroes as soldiers with the pay and rations of volunteers, is going on in this district with no great success."[1] One of Montgomery's men who went with him to South Carolina remembered the doubts with which the Southern Negroes received the abolitionist colonel from Kansas. One day the colonel appeared at a religious meeting the Negroes were having outdoors. This, he thought, would be a fine time for filling the ranks of his Second South Carolina Regiment. The Negroes, however, were "very suspicious and evasive." They were armed with clubs and they "looked bad." The situation called for resourcefulness, but the hymn-singing, scripture-quoting colonel called out to the restless crowd saying, "Let us pray." Then with a barrel for a pulpit he invoked the aid of Heaven "with his eyes closed, and when he opened them all suspicions and all clubs were gone and the Negroes rushed to enlist."[2]

Enthusiasm and zeal soon diminished however. "Their courage oozed out of their fingers' ends and the company could scarcely turn out a corporal's guard." There was no evidence of sustained loyalty among the Negroes. In the opinion of one observer the "contrabands" had "no heart for the business when they reflected upon the possibility of being punctured by cold steel, or perforated by bullets."[3] Nevertheless, Montgomery's persistence and religious appeal won out and he finally secured a regiment of runaway slaves and captives to carry out depredations against the Southern planters.

After Montgomery had filled the ranks of the Second South Carolina, he and Colonel Higginson carried their Negroes to Jacksonville, Florida, to assist in the capture of that city at the mouth of the St. Johns River. As they sailed down the coast Colonel Higginson wrote General Saxton on February 1 from the steamer *Ben De Ford,* saying they took what supplies they found useful on

---

[1] *The New York Herald,* May 16, 1862.

[2] *Ibid.*

[3] *Ibid.*

stops in Georgia at St. Simons and Jekyll Island and at the town of St. Marys.[4] The object of the expedition was to occupy Jacksonville and make it a base of operations for forays up and down the river in search of more Negroes. Arming them, they planned to use them in taking over the entire state. Montgomery went up the St. Johns as far as Palatka, about seventy-five miles south of Jacksonville, raiding that place on April 12. Soon after, General Saxton wrote from Beaufort, South Carolina to Secretary of War Stanton saying, "It gives me pleasure to report that so far the objects of the expedition have been fully accomplished."[5] Colonel John D. Rust of the Eighth Maine Volunteers gave Colonel Halpine at the Hilton Head base an account of the Palatka raid. He said, "Colonel Montgomery, with about 120 men of his regiment, accompanied by Captain Steedman, of the gunboat *Paul Jones*, made a successful expedition . . . taking prisoners, a lieutenant, and 14 men, with all their arms . . ." He also reported property captured such as cotton, rifles, and horses.[6] Confederate Captain J. J. Dickison thought "the illustrious colonel" had been wounded on this expedition.[7] If this were true, it was not a serious wound because the "illustrious" Jayhawker was very much alive and continued to harass the Southern coast with increasing vigor.

Darien had a second taste of Yankee shells in the middle of May. A New York paper, the *Herald*, quoted the Savannah *Daily News* of May 17 as saying, "Two Yankees steamers opened fire with shot and shell on Darien Friday."[8] No damage had been reported, but the *Herald* was doubtful of the veracity of the Southern paper and thought that perhaps, after all, some damage might have been done. In any case, such disruption of Darien's normal life as had been taking place ever since the Yankees arrived caused some of the Darien people to flee, some refugeeing as far away as Macon and Milledgeville. By the spring of 1862 so many had left the town that Pastor Francis Robert Goulding's Presbyterian congregation had not held a service since the ninth of March.[9]

Colonel Higginson occupied Jacksonville while Montgomery made his way back to Hilton Head. The praying colonel from Kansas needed more Negroes to fill the ranks of his regiment than he could get in Florida, and was back in South Carolina to recruit additional black fighters. A circular was

---

[4]*OR: Armies*, ser. I, vol. 14, p. 196.

[5]Saxton to Stanton, Mar. 14, 1863, *ibid.*, ser. I, vol 14, p. 226.

[6]*Ibid.*

[7]*Ibid.*

[8]*The New York Herald*, May 29, 1863.

[9]Darien Presybterian Church Records.

issued at McPhersonville on May 29 warning the tidewater people that the Kansas Jayhawker was back and planning forays from his Hilton Head base. The circular quoted the New York *Tribune* as saying, "Negro troops . . . will soon start upon an expedition under the command of Colonel Montgomery, different from any heretofore projected . . . and it would be well to be on the lookout."[10] This was the sensational raid up the Combahee which took place on June 1-2, 1863.

Some of Montgomery's earlier raids had garnered more poultry and pigs than Negroes. Higginson thought the Kansas colonel had elevated the river raids to "the dignity of a fine art," and confessed that they were "more Western and liberal" than he was accustomed to. He described one such raid: "I remember being on the wharf with some naval officers when [Montgomery] came down from his first trip. The steamer seemed an animated hen-coop. Live poultry hung from the foremost shrouds, dead ones from the mainmast, geese hissed from the binnacle, a pig paced the quarterdeck, and a duck's wings were seen fluttering from a line which was wont to sustain duck trousers."[11]

Joining Montgomery's Second South Carolina Regiment on the Combahee raid was the Third Rhode Island Battery. The troops, white and colored, boarded the transport steamers *Harriet A. Weed,* and *Sentinel,* and the *John Adams,* a sailing sloop mounting eight guns. During the first two days of June they penetrated the South Carolina mainland for twenty miles by way of the Combahee River. The South Carolinians had erected defenses at Fields Point and Tar Bluff, but Montgomery's force drove them out and moved up the river to the summer resort town of Ashepoo, destroying rice plantations and stored rice and cotton.

Montgomery was competely successful on this expedition. It resulted in the seizure of about eight hundred Negroes and other spoils, and in the destruction of an estimated two million dollars worth of property.[12] The success of the raid was due to the effectiveness of a Negress, Harriet Tubman, a Union scout and spy whom the Negroes called "Moses." Harriet, with several men to help her, organized and led the raid for Colonel Montgomery.[13] She and her spy squad helped the Western colonel on a number of raids from South Carolina to Florida, but the Combahee river raid was the most successful of them all. In the words of the Boston *Commonwealth,* the seizure of so much property and the

---

[10]*OR: Armies,* Ser. 1, vol. 14, p. 307.

[11]Thomas Wentworth Higginson, *Army Life in a Black Regiment* (Boston, 1870), p. 114.

[12]*The New York Times,* June 19, 1863.

[13]Earl Conrad, *Harriet Tubman* (Washington, 1943), p. 168.

destruction of cotton and stores was "a glorious consummation."[14] Sarah Bradford in a little book narrating the experiences of Harriet, tells how the Negroes came running down to the river from their quarters, and from their work in the fields, eight hundred of them coming down every road, women with pails on their heads, children on their backs and hanging onto their dresses. Some women carried pigs. Harriet said one woman had two pigs, one white and one black which they named Beauregard and Jeff Davis respectively. Down to the river bank they rushed. Small boats quickly filled with Negroes, babies, pigs, and possessions and put off to the "Lincoln gun-boats" in the middle of the river. They were struggling to get on the small boats all at once. The oarsmen tried to beat them off to keep the boats from overloading, but the Negroes seized the little boats and would not let go. Montgomery called from the upper deck of the gun boat saying, "Moses, you'll have to give them a song." Harriet then raised her voice and sang:

> Of all the whole creation in the East or the West,
> The glorious Yankee nation is the greatest and the best.
> Come along! Come along! don't be alarmed
> Uncle Sam is rich enough to give you a farm[15].

The Negroes, exhilarated by the singing, threw up their hands in joyous ecstasy as they shouted "Glory!" Then the boats freed from their grasp moved off without them.

A New York *Times* reporter described the Combahee raid: "The surprise was complete, interrupting without ceremony the social machinery of the Southerners." Colonel William C. Heyward, the officer who had lost Fort Walker to the invader in November, 1861, lost again to the Yankees. This time "a fine horse to Colonel Montgomery and a pair of silver-mounted holsters and pistols."[16] The reporter worked himself up to a dramatic pitch as he described the darkies weeping for joy at their liberation. One old Negro "bowing to every white face with streaming eyes and clasped hands, cried, 'Bless de Lord, de day hab come at last—de day hab come at last!' "[17]

---

[14] *The* (Boston) *Commonwealth*, July 10, 1863, as quoted in Conrad, p. 169.

[15] Sarah H. Bradford, *Harriet, The Moses of Her People* (New York, 1886). Conrad also relates this incident (pp. 174-175).

[16] *The New York Times*, June 19, 1863.

[17] *Ibid.*

V

BLACK YANKEES IN BLUE COATS

During The chilly winter month of January, 1863, while Montgomery was leaving the ice and snow of battle-scarred Kansas for the warmer clime of South Carolina, Harvard-bred Robert Gould Shaw was invited to organize a regiment of Negro troops and to take them South to help liberate their own people from the bonds of slavery. The invitation came from the governor of Massachusetts, Shaw's home state. Governor John Albion Andrew was of strong abolitionist sentiments, the chief executive of a state which had nourished a large number of leading abolitionists, and he became enthusiastic over the idea of organizing a regiment of Negroes to go to the South. Having sought and obtained authorization from the Secretary of War to do this, he wrote to Francis G. Shaw who had moved from Boston to Staten Island, New York offering to make his son its colonel.[1] Robert had been in Virginia serving as aide-de-camp to General George Henry Gordon in the Shenandoah Valley. He had passed unharmed through several engagements, including the Battle of Winchester. This had prepared him to command troops in the field. Governor Andrew's letter complimented Robert and expressed confidence in his ability to lead the regiment which the Governor would designate as the Fifty-Fourth Massachusetts Volunteers. For this first Negro regiment ever recruited in the

---

[1]John A. Andrew to Francis G. Shaw, Jan. 30, 1863. Quoted in Luis F. Emilio, *History of the Fifty-Fourth Regiment of Massachusetts Volunteers Infantry, 1863-1865* (Boston, 1894), 3.

North the Governor wanted, in his own words, "white officers of firm anti-slavery principles, ambitious, superior to a vulgar contempt for color, and having faith in the capacity of colored men for military service."[2] Enclosed was a letter to Robert officially requesting his service in this unique venture.

Robert Shaw was born in Boston in 1837 of a prominent family of that city. He was the only son of a father who was closely identified with the New England Abolitionists.[3] His mother, Sarah Blake Sturgis Shaw, was also an ardent humanitarian interested in the abolition of Negro slavery. Robert was educated at home and abroad in his early years, then was admitted to Harvard in 1856. After three years he discontinued his studies and went to New York City where he entered the mercantile business of Henry P. Sturgis, his mother's brother.[4] The outbreak of war interrupted his short business career and he volunteered for military service. On April 19, 1861, he went with his regiment, the Seventh New York National Guard, to defend the nation's capital. One of his subordinates said of him, "His bearing was graceful, as became a soldier and gentleman. His family connections were of the highest social standing, character, and influence." Peter Burchard, his biographer, described him as "handsome . . . intelligent, sensitive" but not sentimental, . . . "a soldier of unquestionable bravery," as a person, "charming." He had an "easy manner" and a "lively disposition."[5] Robert's friend, Charles Russell Lowell, described him as "slight of frame, with a gentle, almost schoolgirlish charm that inspired affectionate admiration and caused women to think how proud [of him] his mother must be."[6] And Charlotte Forten, a mulatto teacher from Philadelphia who had common interest with Shaw in the Port Royal Experiment carried on by Northern humanitarians, spoke of him as "our noble, beautiful young colonel."[7] In an attempt to offset the youthful, "school-girlish" look he had now

---

[2]*Ibid.*

[3]*Ibid.*, 4.

[4]Peter Burchard, *One Gallant Rush* (New York, 1965), 21. Burchard goes into detail concerning Shaw's early life, family background, and the Abolitionist influences surrounding him.

[5]Emilio, 4., Burchard, 3.

[6]Quoted in Willie Lee Rose, *Rehearsal for Reconstruction: The Port Royal Experiment* (Indianapolis, New York, Kansas City, 1964), 250.

[7]Quoted in Burchard, 146. The Port Royal Experiment was the early wartime Reconstruction effort by which Northerners educated the liberated slaves of that area and attempted to make responsible citizens of them. This is treated fully in Rose, *Rehearsal for Reconstruction.*

grown a mustache and chin whiskers, making him even more attractive to the women.

The Governor's offer placed Robert in a quandary. Should he accept it? Could a regiment of Negroes be trained to become an effective fighting force? Were there enough free Negroes in Massachusetts, or in the North for that matter, willing to fight for the liberation of their brothers down South? What would be the problems of discipline? Would there be glory and honor for himself, for his Negroes, for his country? It is not known whether or not his father advised him one way or another, but Robert himself had to make the final decision. Sarah, his mother, waited anxiously as Robert weighed the matter. She hoped very much that he would accept the command. If she could have had a premonition of things to come she might have tried to persuade him not to run the risk of death, but her humanitarian sentiments outweighed her fears for him and she could not help urging him to do what she felt was right. She knew he would be ridiculed and perhaps die; but death was always a possibility for a soldier, and as for ridicule she would convert that to honor. Death in such a cause would be a badge of honor in her eyes and in the eyes of her antislavery friends. Brother officers often scorned white men who led Negro troops. West Pointers were especially scornful of such officers as Shaw, Higginson, and General N. P. Banks.[8] But the Abolitionists thought of them as courageous crusaders for freedom. Later the Confederate Congress passed a law which permitted military courts to order the death penalty for any captured white officers who commanded Negroes "in arms against the Confederate States."[9] But even if he must pay with his life, the cause was one to demand her son's full measure of devotion. Sarah Shaw accepted vicariously the martyr's role. Robert hesitated for a little while, but by February 15 he was in Boston with his answer. He would accept the command.[10]

---

[8]John Hope Franklin, *From Slavery to Freedom*... 3rd edition (New York, 1967), pp. 290-291.

[9]The act reads as follows: "That every white person being a commissioned officer, or acting as such, who during the present war, shall command Negroes or Mulattoes in arms against the Confederate States, or who shall arm, train, organize, or prepare Negroes or Mulattoes for military service against the Confederate States, or who shall voluntarily aid Negroes or Mulattoes in any military enterprise, attack, or conflict in such service, [shall], if captured, be put to death, or be otherwise punished at the discretion of the court." Act of May 1, 1863, 3rd Session of the 1st Congress, 1863. James M. Matthews, editor, *Statutes at Large of the Confederate States of America*... (Richmond, 1863), p. 168. See also W. B. Yearns, *The Confederate Congress* (Athens, 1960), p. 164.

[10]Emilio, p. 5.

The next several weeks were busy ones. The job of recruiting, organizing, and drilling the Fifty-Fourth Massachusetts Volunteer Infantry Regiment, Colored, was not as easy as the Governor in his enthusiam for this novel idea might have thought; but the young Colonel—he was only twenty-five years old—proved worthy of the trust that had been placed in him.

Not only was Shaw himself busy recruiting Negroes for his regiment but others were assisting, even beyond the bounds of the state. His subordinate officers, the Hollowell brothers, were among those busily engaged in recruiting. Governor Andrew had first made Norwood lieutenant colonel of the Fifty-Fourth and later colonel of the Fifty-Fifth Massachusetts, another Negro regiment, and had made his brother Edward major, and then lieutenant colonel, of the Fifty-Fourth. Edward did some recruiting in Philadelphia, not officially, of course, but effective nevertheless. The Abolitionist leaders, seeing that they would have to take Negroes outside of Massachusetts, formed a "Black Committee," appointed by Governor Andrew, whose duty it was to supervise the raising of Negro troops. Robert's father served on this committee.[11]

While Montgomery was making himself feared by the planters of the South Atlantic tidewater region, General David Hunter, commanding the Department of the South from Hilton Head, decided he wanted more Negroes to harass the area, more than runaway slaves could supply. He had heard of the effort of Governor Andrew to raise a regiment of Massachusetts Negroes, and on May 18 asked the War Department to send the Fifty-Fourth regiment to him. The War Department responded by instructing the Governor to send this regiment to Hilton Head at once.[12]

Governor Andrew wanted to give the Fifty-Fourth a glorious send-off. A great crowd gathered at the regiment's training camp at Readville to hear the Governor speak and to present the appropriate flags. The Star Spangled Banner was presented by the young colored lads of Boston, another national flag was presented by the Colored Ladies Relief Society, and the regimental flag was presented by "friends of the regiment."[13] Perhaps the two most prominent Negroes in Colonel Shaw's regiment were Lewis and Charles Douglass, sons of Frederick Douglass, the well-known Negro who had risen from slavery to become an Abolitionist editor.

The ceremonies were impressive. After a prayer by a Reverend Grimes the

---

[11]Burchard, p. 77; Rose, p. 249.

[12]Emilio, p. 31.

[13]*The New York Times,* May 19, 1863.

regiment formed "in a hollow square" and Governor Andrew presented the flags. The Governor spoke of the exceptional character of the regiment as marking an era in the history of the war, the Commonwealth, the country, and humanity . . ."[14] Colonel Shaw made a "soldier-like response"[15] in which he said, "May we show you that you have not made a mistake in intrusting the honor of the State to a colored regiment."[16] Secretly he hoped his Negroes would not disappoint him. He knew full well that the real test lay ahead, and only time would tell whether his Negroes would fight or run under fire. Twenty thousand people gathered to see the Fifty-Fourth march away to Battery Wharf, whence the troops sailed on the *De Molay* to Southern waters.[17]

William Lloyd Garrison, with his hand upon a bust of John Brown, watched from the balcony at Wendell Phillips's Essex Street home as the regiment marched by.[18] Brown's spirit was there too, though his body lay a-moldering in the ground, while James Montgomery, his counterpart and Jayhawk friend of Kansas days, was waiting off the Georgia coast to welcome Shaw and his black troops. Sad, but proud to tell this young colonel goodbye, were his mother and his bride. They, too, and his sisters watched the parade of the black regiment, watched from the second story balcony of his mother's childhood home on Beacon Street. Robert had married Annie Kneeland Haggerty earlier that month in the Church of the Ascension in New York City.[19] Now he must leave his bride and sail away with his regiment on its unique mission.

---

[14]*Ibid.*

[15]*Ibid.*

[16]Emilio, p. 30.

[17]See Saunders Redding, "Tonight for Freedom," *American Heritage,* June, 1958, p. 53.

[18]The Massachusetts Historical Society has verified the fact that Wendell Phillips had a bust of John Brown in his home. It was probably done by Edward Augustus Brackett. See letter to SBK Jr. May 24, 1960.

[19]Burchard, p. 93.

VI

FLAME OF HATE

COLONEL SHAW'S orders were to bring the Fifty-Fourth to St. Simons Island. There he would meet Colonel Montgomery. This island lies off the Georgia coast at the mouth of the Altamaha River. After brief pauses at Beaufort and Hilton Head, the *De Molay* landed the black regiment at the southern end of the island early on Tuesday morning, June 9. Shaw's nine hundred Negroes had sung their John Brown song most of the way down the Southern coast from Hilton Head. Several of the officers went ashore immediately. One of them described Thomas Butler King's plantation which he visited. It was "a splendid place." The tropical plants and flowers attracted his attention. He could see such a sight at home "only in hot houses," while on this island they were "so abundantly and luxuriantly spread before you, that you are lost in wonder and delight." He thought the live oaks with their gray dripping moss "the most magnificent spectacle of all."[1] McIntosh County was where John and William Bartram, many years before, had found a flowering tree which William named the *Franklinia Altamaha* in honor of Benjamin Franklin. It was found on an old Indian trail a few miles northwest of Darien near the Barrington Road. It had become known as the *Lost Gordonia,* having disappeared by 1903.[2] But on

---

[1] *Rebellion Record,* 1863 (New York, 1864), 296. Filed in Special Collections, University of Georgia Libraries, Athens, Georgia.

[2] Bartram at first thought the tree was a species of Gardonia but upon determining that it was not of that genus he gave this "head of a new tribe" the name Franklinia

the islands and the mainland around Darien officers and men of the Fifty-Fourth could still see and marvel at the beauty of the green cassina, the azalea, tea olive, cherry laurel, and japonica, the bay, magnolia, the fragrant jessamine and many other beautiful plants that flourish there.

As for the colonels of the black regiments, there was very little similarity between them. Montgomery, approaching his fiftieth year, was twice Shaw's age. The two men were vastly different in heritage, and in their meeting there was no real comradeship. Nothing could have drawn them together other than the purpose that brought them both to this place. They were both Abolitionists, they both wanted to see the slaves set free and were willing to lead their Negroes in this effort; but here the likeness ended. Dr. Seth Rogers, of the Medical Department in Colonel Higginson's regiment, in writing to his daughter described Colonel Montgomery as having slightly rounded shoulders, as being tall, slender and dark with a bronzed face, as having a Roman nose, heavy beard and mustache, a small determined mouth and pointed chin, and "deep hazel eyes of destiny."[3] Higginson thought Montgomery himself was equal to one whole regiment. Rogers remembered how Colonel Montgomery once ordered five rebel prisoners shot to avenge the death of five of his soldiers who were taken prisoners and shot by the rebels. To Rogers he seemed to be "one of the John Brown men of destiny."[4] And Robert Shaw himself in a letter to Annie wrote: "Montgomery is a strange compound; he allows no swearing or drinking in his regiment, and is anti-tobacco; but he burns and destroys wherever he goes with great gusto and looks as if he would have quite a taste for hanging people, whenever a suitable subject should offer."[5]

Now these two colonels met at the mouth of the river that flows by the little town of Darien. Soon they would travel up that river to share an awful moment of partnership in the destruction of homes and sacred places of worship.

Colonel Montgomery had received a dispatch from General Hunter on June 9, the day of Shaw's arrival, instructing him to "spare all household furniture, libraries, churches, and hospitals."[6] In his orders to Montgomery, General Hunter enclosed a set of "Instructions for Government of the Armies

---

Altamaha, *The Travels of William Bartram.* Edited by Mark Van Doren (New York, 1928), p. 369.

[3]Letter of February 24, 1863. Massachusetts Historical Society, *Proceedings,* vol. 43, p. 367.

[4]*Ibid.*

[5]Quoted in Burchard, p. 101.

[6]*OR: Armies,* ser. I, vol. 14, p. 467.

of the United States in the Field" which had been prepared by Francis Lieber and issued by the War Department on April 24, 1863. One section stated that "all destruction of property not commanded by the authorized officer [is] prohibited under penalty of death . . ."[7] But the commanding general hinted that harsh measures might be justified. It was his opinion that "the wickedness and folly of the enemy" might require "the stern necessity of retaliation."[8] Montgomery knew a lot about retaliation. He had learned it from experience in Kansas, and he had learned how to apply it effectively both in Kansas and on the Atlantic coast. Now he would teach the young Massachusetts colonel how to apply it at Darien. An order from General Hunter issued on June 10 gave Montgomery added incentive to impress upon Colonel Shaw the necessity of severe measures of retaliation. The commanding general had been considerably disturbed by the Confederate law which demanded the death penalty for officers who were leading Negroes in arms against the Confederacy.

Hunter was very specific: "Colonel," he ordered, "Every rebel man you may capture, citizen or soldier, you will send in irons to this place to be kept as hostages [sic] for the proper treatment of any of your men who may accidentally fall into the hands of the enemy."[9] Montgomery was very receptive to the idea. Once after ordering five prisoners shot he refused to permit ten others to take an oath of allegiance to the United States but sent them back to join their troops with the message that he would not be content with a life for a life but would take "ten for one if they persisted in their hellish career of atrocity."[10]

Montgomery had been to Brunswick on the mainland and had returned to St. Simons Island with General Hunter's orders. Spotting Colonel Shaw on the Wharf, the older man asked, "How soon can you start on an expedition?"

"In half an hour," Robert replied.

After all, had he not spent months in preparation for this sort of thing and traveled all the way from Boston to test his Negroes' ability to stike a massive blow for the freedom of their race? Colonel Shaw was eager to give his colored troops some exercise. Inactivity was not good for them. They had grown restless.

The expedition consisted of five companies of Montgomery's Second South Carolina and eight of Shaw's Fifty-Fourth, plus the Third Rhode Island

---

[7]*Ibid.*, ser. III, vol. 3, p. 153.

[8]*Ibid.*

[9]*Ibid.*, ser. II, vol. 5, p. 770.

[10]Seth Rogers, in Massachusetts Historical Society, *Proceedings*, XL., 367.

Battery.[11] Hurried preparations were made and men of the Fifty-Fourth boarded the *Sentinel*. Other ships, the *John Adams*, the *Paul Jones*, and the *Harriet A. Weed*, also joined the expedition. The *Sentinel* entered Doboy Sound at sunrise. Then, joined by the others, she sailed up the Darien River. The gunboats came within sight of the town, shelling houses along the way. Alligators, excited by the noise, flapped and rolled in the mucky water. A frightened marsh hen flew up from her watery nest, and sea gulls wheeled high above the clouds of smoke.

There were in the town about eighty homes, five churches, twelve stores, a few mills and storehouses containing rice, resin, and turpentine. In addition, there was a court house, a jail, and a school house. The main street, shaded by large and beautiful mulberry trees and moss-draped live oaks, ran parallel to the river. Darien had been a town of over five hundred whites and three times as many Negroes. But now most of the townspeople who had not already refugeed to places far away were on the Ridge, three miles north of town. The migration of people from Darien had become heavier as a consequence of the coastal raids in 1862.[12] So depleted were the churches that the Reverend Samuel Pinkerton held no more services at St. Andrews Episcopal Church and the Reverend Francis Goulding's Presbyterian flock had been scattered since March.[13] The migration had begun in earnest in the spring. The Pease family had a summer home which they called "The Thicket." Taking whatever they could of things they thought they would need they had left with other refugeeing families in the mass exodus. Augusta rode horseback, her mother rode on top of the loaded wagon and the servants walked alongside. Three of Augusta's girl companions were visiting her and the McIntosh Cavalry as a compliment to the young ladies paraded in full uniform. A lookout for the blockading Yankees could see them through his spyglass and reported it to his commander. As soon as the tide rose the Union boats approached and threw shells at the house. The family and visitors fled. Augusta said a shell struck a tree at the corner of the house and "so great was the shock my bird cage door flew open and the birds were free".[14]

The Darien people on the Ridge needed badly now those stalwart Scots whom Oglethorpe had brought over long ago. Families and neighbors huddled

---

[11]*Rebellion Record*, 295.

[12]A Macon lady, now deceased, had a four-poster bed which if it could talk would tell an interesting tale of a long and difficult wagon journey from Darien in flight from Yankee marauders. She was the late Mabel Harris, longtime principal of Alexander II School, Macon, Ga.

[13]Records of these two churches show no services from this time until after the war.

[14]Augusta I. Pease to "Mrs. Atwood". Atlanta, Sept. 13, 1901.

together like chickens frightened by a hawk. Only a small company of about twenty soldiers under the command of Captain W. A. Lane stood between them and the Negro troops in the town.[15] Most all of the able-bodied men of the South had left in 'sixty-one either with the McIntosh Guards, the McIntosh Cavalry, or Captain Brailford's company.

As the *John Adams* approached the wharf she continued to pour shot and shell into the town. What few inhabitants remained ran terror-stricken in every direction.[16] When Montgomery was told that there was a strong force of cavalry "just five miles away," he did not even bother to verify that information but marched "nearly his whole force into the town, posted his sentries and prepared to do his work."[17] About four hundred Negro soldiers participated in looting the town.[18] One of the officers described the pillaging: "The men began to come in by twos, threes, and dozens, loaded with every species and all sort and quantities of furniture, stores, trinkets, and such, until one would be tired of enumerating. We had sofas, tables, pianos, chairs, mirrors, carpets, beds, carpenter's tools, books, china sets, tinware, Confederate shinplasters, old letters, papers . . ." Much turpentine and resin was seized. Chickens and livestock were added to the cargo piling up on the wharf to be loaded on the Yankee boats. With the rice and corn which was taken there was enough food to feed Montgomery's men for "at least a month."[19] What cows and calves that were not taken on board were shot and left dead in the streets, according to one eyewitness.[20] Nor was there room on the boats for horses which suffered the same fate. After a few days decaying animal flesh would cause a stench that would reach the Ridge with the wind blowing in that direction.

When the few remaining citizens had been driven out and all the loot that could be taken had been stored on board the boats, Montgomery told Shaw he wanted to burn the town.[21] Robert protested, told Montgomery he did not want to take the responsibility of burning a defenseless town for no good

---

[15]See Lane's Report, *OR: Armies*, ser. I, vol. 14, p. 318.

[16]*Rebellion Record*, 295.

[17]*Ibid.*

[18]*Emilio*, 42.

[19]*Rebellion Record*, 295.

[20]*Daily Morning News* (Savannah), June 16, 1863.

[21]Robert Shaw to Sarah Blake Shaw, June 12, 1863, as quoted in Mrs. Shaw's letter, Aug. 29, 1870, to Robert R. Clute, rector of St. Andrews Episcopal Church, Darien, Ga. Typed copy in possession of Thomas H. Gignilliat, Savannah, Ga. Original lost. See Preface.

reason; but Montgomery said he would be glad to take it on is own shoulders.[22]

"Why should I not burn it?" he asked. "I could tell you stories about the misdeeds of slave owners that would make your hair stand on end."

One experience vivid in his memory was of the night in Kansas when a Bushwhacker had taken a shot at him through a rifle opening in his fort. The attacker had gotten a bead on a candle flame through the opening. The bullet had flattened against one of the rafters above the bed near his wife's side as she lay there half frozen in fear.[23] Again he recalled how one night his enemies had set fire to his wagon loaded with hay and had let it roll down the hill toward the fort, veering away at the last moment.[24]

Shaw had no such memories, but he had been deeply imbued with abolitionism through reading poems of Whittier, Lowell, and other New England poets and through listening to the orations of Wendell Phillips. His parents in their Boston home had frequently entertained such ardent reformers as these and other strong Abolitionists, men such as Sumner, Parker, Garrison. And they were close friends of Fanny Kemble, the well-known English actress who had tried the life of a planter's wife and found it distasteful in the extreme.[25] Colonel Shaw's own father, in fact, had secured the copyright for Miss Kemble's plantation journal, published under the title *Journal of a Residence on a Georgia Plantation*.[26] In it she thoroughly castigated the slave owners. In spite of all the antislavery environment and influence in his life, however, the New England Colonel could not bring himself to condone the Kansas Colonel's extreme acts of vengeance.

Even as he protested the burning of this defenseless town, he may have remembered how when he was in Virginia the Confederates had burned the town of Hampton, destroying that refuge for liberated slaves. In any case, he did, though reluctantly, order Company I of his regiment to aid Montgomery's

---

[22] *Ibid.*

[23] Mitchell, p. 19. Clarinda Evans of Licking Valley, Mo. Montgomery had two children by a former marriage. Clarinda reared them and bore her husband eight more, six of whom lived to maturity. See *Ibid.*, p. 28.

[24] *Ibid.*

[25] See Burchard, p. 3.

[26] Frances Anne Kemble's book, *Journal of a Residence on a Georgia Plantation in 1838-1839*, was deposited by Francis G. Shaw in the Clerk's Office of the District Court of the Southern District of New York on June 6, 1863, and his right of proprietorship was asserted. Office of the Register of Copyrights, Copyright Office, The Library of Congress, Nov. 20, 1867.

Negroes in their work of destruction. Further evidence that indicates Shaw might have objected to what was going on is seen in an item which appeared in the *New York Times* soon after the incident: "The enterprise would have accomplished more but for the strange misconduct on the part of the transport *Sentinel.*" This was the steamer which carried Shaw's officers and men. The reporter said, "The officers . . . have since been put upon a course of discipline which, it is hoped, will work some improvement either in their loyalty or their courage."[27]

One of the invaders described the devastation of Darien: "It was a beautiful town, and never did look so both grand and beautiful as in its destruction. As soon as a house was ransacked, the match was applied, and by six o'clock the whole town was in one sheet of flame. It was a magnificent spectacle, but still very few were found to gloat over it. Had we had a hard fight to gain the place, or had we taken a thousand slaves by its destruction, we would have had no complaints. And I suppose we should have none anyway. The South must be conquered inch by inch, and what we can't put a force in to hold ought to be destroyed. If we must burn the South out, so be it."[28]

As the flames licked the evening sky the black smoke mixed and blended with the red glow of sunset and fire. What turpentine and resin that had not been seized in the looting had been ignited causing smoke and flame to belch toward the heavens. The school, the churches, and private homes represented one kind of loss suffered by the Darien people, the business places represented another. The Darien Dispensary, the saloons, the Boot and Shoe Manufactory, the Saddler and Harness Shop, the Clock and Watch Maker, book stores, the apothecary shop, all means of livelihood were disrupted or destroyed in the fire. Gone, too, were the jail and the court house, and with them all legal protection, and for awhile all semblance of justice. The fire could not purify the town and the foul odors of rotting offal and burning animal flesh was a constant reminder to the refugees on the Ridge of the extent of the destruction of their town and the desecration of their places of worship.

A Southern planter was considered rich if he owned property worth as much as $20,000. Planters in McIntosh County who in the Census of 1860 listed the value of their real and personal property in that range, and some as high as $150,000, were among the county's more prosperous men at that time. By this standard, the heavy losers to the Yankee spoilers were William Cook, D. M. Dunwoody, Norman and Robert Gignilliat, Charles H. Hopkins, Michael J. Kenan, Reuben King, Frank McDonald, Charles and Randolph Spalding, and

---

[27] *The New York Times,* June 23, 1863.

[28] *Rebellion Record,* 297.

Alexander W. Wylly. Theo P. Pease and Jacob Rokenbaugh were timber men worth well over $1000,000 each. Alexander Mitchell was one of the rich merchants of Darien, listing his real and personal property at $58,000. And over the county line in Glynn, among the heaviest losers were the Kings, the Coopers, and the Troups. Butler's Island, deserted during the war, was never again to see the prosperity of the days when the Pierce Butlers produced rice there with slaves which Fanny Kemble abhorred with such passion. Frances Butler and her father came down from Philadelphia at war's end and tried to revive the plantation but he soon died, leaving to her the impossible task. All these and more lost their cotton, their rice, their thousands of slaves, and their hundreds of thousands of dollars in property loss. William B. Charters was not among the wealthy, but was a young blacksmith from Nova Scotia. He, too, was a loser with no forge now at which to practice his trade. But dead horses have no use for shoes, and the stolen horses would now be shod by smithes who had learned their trade "under the spreading chestnut tree."

Colonel Shaw's conscience must have begun to prick him as he discussed the burning of Darien with his fellow officers. But Montgomery said he wanted Southerners to "feel that this was a real war."[29] Such statements were not surprising to those who knew this Abolitionist from Kansas and who knew of his escapades in the Kansas civil war. Lieutenant John Gray, who had been Shaw's friend at Harvard, wrote to his sister in Boston saying, "Colonel Montgomery is cordially detested by everybody."[30] Western Jayhawkers were as distasteful as were Southern slave holders to some New Englanders. To Lieutenant Gray, such a man as Montgomery was one "who hates slavery because it is an institution belonging to his neighbor over the border with whom he has always been carrying on barbarous and bloody warfare."

The town having been destroyed, the *Harriet A. Weed*, one of the boats of the expedition, went up the river in search of a Confederate boat which was reported to have had a cargo of long staple cotton well worth the taking. The craft was located four miles up the river. It was a large flat-boat, a copper-bottomed schooner, loaded with eighty bales of the prized cotton valued at thirty thousand dollars. As the *Harriet A. Weed* returned with its spoils to St. Simons the soldiers and crew were greeted with "nine tremendous cheers" by the Massachusetts and South Carolina Negroes.[31]

After the invaders had completed their work of sacking and burning and

---

[29]Emilio, p. 42.

[30]*War Letters of John Chipman Gray and John Codman Ropes, 1862-1865* (Boston, 1927), 232.

[31]*Rebellion Record*, 295.

had settled themselves comfortably with their loot on St. Simons Island, citizens who had been on the Ridge began to come back to examine the damage. They came hoping to find something that might be salvaged from the smoking ruins. Instead, they found the town "one plain of ashes and of blackened chimneys." One of them said there were but "three small houses left," plus the Methodist church which had been set on fire but did not burn.[32] Another, on returning to the scene said, "It is a sad sight to see smoking ruins now ... For myself I feel this calamity severely. You know I have lost heavily since the war commenced, but I had still a good home left. This is now also gone."[33] Another lamented, "And to think it was burned by the cowardly Yankee Negro thieves."[34] One of the women viewing the wreckage exclaimed, "It was a cowardly wanton outrage!"[35]

The great mills that had once sawed lumber to be shipped all over the world were a part of the wreckage. The docks that shortly before had stretched for nearly three miles fronting the town were deserted. The booms that had held logs so numerous that a man could walk across the river on them were empty. Where now were the stores, the shops and the saloons? Where could the people gather for social and religious meetings? Where would the little children go to learn their letters and do their sums? The streets were lined with ghost-like scorched mulberry trees and oaks shrouded with singed moss. For the fainthearted all was hopelessness; for the courageous, a challenge.

On the day after the destruction of Darien, General Hunter had a visitor at Hilton Head. He was Brigadier General Quincy A. Gillmore, and he brought with him orders that instructed him to replace Hunter as the commander of the Department of the South. Although the change in command was planned before the burning of Darien, it came after earlier raids and burnings of a similar nature. Shaw had already heard rumors that Hunter might be removed for allowing Montgomery too much leeway in his utter disregard of property rights.[36]

Hunter and his adjutant, Halpine, alias poet Miles O'Reilly, sailed from Port Royal on the *Arago* on Sunday, June 15. They arrived in New York the following Tuesday morning with nearly six hundred fellow passengers.[37] The ship docked and the two officers went ashore.

---

[32] *Daily Morning News* (Savannah), June 16, 1863.

[33] *Ibid.*

[34] *Ibid.*

[35] *Ibid.*

[36] Burchard, p. 99.

[37] *The New York Times*, June 18, 1863.

"There is something good about this after all," Hunter said to Halpine as they walked down the gangplank.

"What is that?", asked the adjutant.

"Getting away from the heat and all the pests that come with summer, and the damned sand that we had to endure year round, sand in our shoes, in our hair, in our food. And getting away from all those cringing niggers who swarmed around, always under foot."

Then, as an afterthought he added, "It's good that we could leave Sambo there to stop the bullet meant for you."

"That's a gruesome thought, and you should not have said it," said Halpine, half scolding.

"I didn't, you said it in that silly poem you wrote back at Hilton Head," was Hunter's parting shot as they separated.

After his return to the North, General Hunter inquired of the President if he were being removed as a reprimand for ravaging undefended coastal towns. The President tactfully denied it.[38] However, since he did not give Hunter a clear reason for his removal, one wonders if it were possible that he had, after all, removed Hunter because he had been waging war against helpless citizens, destroying homes, schools, and churches, and disregarding property rights generally.

Liberating slaves and using them to help Massachusetts Negroes upset the Southern economic and social system might be justified in the minds of Abolitionists of the North and the West, but to use them to destroy defenseless homes and to burn schools and churches could not be condoned by men with a sense of justice. As one Darien citizen put it, "The value in money I would not have thought so much of, as I am getting used to it, but there is something in the word home that puts money out of the question."[39] If there was a humanitarian strain in President Lincoln's character—and this is universally recognized— then he must have removed General Hunter because of the ruthlessness in his department where Negro troops under white officers were looting, pillaging, and burning defenseless villages. Lincoln apparently did not like what Hunter was allowing his subordinates to do. He had revoked Hunter's emancipation order which the general issued soon after taking command of the Southern Department. The President had seen in the order an encouragement of servile insurrection, and he could not bring himself to favor such a radical move. And even after the Emancipation Proclamation had gone into effect he was faced

---

[38] *OR: Armies,* ser. 1, vol. 14, pp. 460, 470.

[39] *Daily Morning News* (Savannah), June 16, 1863.

with the fact that he had let military and diplomatic expediency take precedence over his oath to uphold the Constitution which guaranteed property rights. The pragmatic Lincoln did let the Abolitionists persuade him to issue the proclamation which confiscated slave property of planters who lived in rebel territory regardless of their loyalty or disloyalty to the United States. But victory would mean preservation of the Union, and in the President's mind no price was too high for that. The responsibility for burning Southerners out of their homes might reasonably have been placed on General Hunter. However, Montgomery was the one who ordered the execution of the deed at Darien and Shaw, under orders, reluctantly went along with him.

VII

A MATTER OF CONSCIENCE

O<small>N THE</small> day after the burning of Darien Robert Shaw wrote to his mother telling her about the expedition which ended in the destruction of the undefended little town. The letter expressed not only his abhorrence of the deed but also his denial of responsibility for it. But even as he condemned his fellow officer, one senses, as he reads between the lines, a bothered conscience. The letter was more than a protest expressed in the privacy of correspondence with his mother, it was a confession of his inner thoughts. Deep within himself he shared the shame of it. However, he did not go so far as to take on himself any blame for obeying orders of Colonel Montgomery who, in turn, was under General Hunter's orders. Nevertheless, his humanitarian spirit which had shown so much concern for enslaved black men now rebelled against the inhumane treatment to which their masters were subjected.

"About noon we came in sight of Darien," he wrote. "Montgomery said to me, 'I shall burn this town.' I told him that I did not want the responsibility, and he was only too happy to take it all on his shoulders; so the pretty little place was burned to the ground... One of my companies assisted because he ordered them out, and I had to obey.... The reason he gave me for destroying Darien was that the Southerners must be made to feel that this was a real war, and that they were to be swept away by the hand of God like the Jews of old. In theory this may seem all right to some; but when it comes to being made the instrument of the Lord's vengeance, I myself don't like it."

Then he explained that Montgomery argued that they were not bound by the rules of regular warfare.

"But that makes it none the less revolting to wreak our vengeance on the innocent and defenseless", he said. He was not sure as to what course he should take. Besides his own distaste for "this barbarous kind of warfare," he was "not sure that it will not be very injurious to the reputation of black troops and of those connected with them." "For myself," he continued, "I have gone through the war so far without dishonor, and I do not like to degenerate into a plunderer and a robber; and the same applies to every officer in my regiment. If it were the order of our government to overrun the South with fire and sword, I might look at it in a different light, for then we should be carrying out what had been decided upon as a necessary policy. As the case stands, we are no better than 'Semmes,' who attacks and destroys defenseless vessels." He thought Montgomery was "doing his duty to the best of his knowledge and ability."

He ended his letter by saying, "There are only two courses for me to pursue: To obey orders and say nothing, or to refuse to go on any such expeditions, and be put under arrest—probably court-martialed—which is a serious thing."[1]

Robert's defense of Montgomery seems strange in the light of what he had already learned about the Western colonel. Why would Shaw try to explain Montgomery's conduct by saying he believed he was doing his duty? Duty meant a great deal to both men, of course, trained as they were in army discipline. Could he have felt, as he wrote confidentially to his mother, that the act needed some rational explanation and that the word duty was all he could cling to in an attempt to rationalize it? As the days passed, however, in other letters one sees his unhappiness at the thought of the events of June 11 outweighing any desire to conceal Montgomery's guilt under the cover of obedience to a superior.

His conscience still troubling him, the young colonel wrote to Governor Andrew on June 14 saying, "We met no enemy, and our only exploits were the capture of 85 bales of cotton, and the burning of the town of Darien. The latter disgusted me exceedingly."[2] He went on to say, "I never knew before of a town being burned to the ground without some good reason, especially when it contained only old men, women, and children."[3] The destruction of Darien

[1]Robert Shaw to Sarah Shaw, his mother, June 12, 1863, as quoted in *Harper's Weekly*, Sept. 3, 1870. Mrs. Shaw enclosed a copy of this in her letter to Robert F. Clute, Aug. 29, 1870. Raphael Semmes, referred to in the letter, was the Confederate sea fighter whose flag ship was the *Alabama*.

[2]As quoted in *Harper's Weekly*, Sept. 3, 1870.

[3]*Ibid.*

seemed to him "perfectly useless if not barbarous."[4]

Then on the same day, he made an attempt to determine whether or not Montgomery was really carrying out orders in the burning game or acting on his own authority. Was he, Robert, being used as a tool in a very distasteful act? In an attempt to find out the truth he wrote to Colonel Halpine, the poetic adjutant at Hilton Head: "Has Colonel Montgomery Orders from General Hunter to burn and destroy all towns and dwelling houses he may capture?" Then he declared, "If he does this on his own responsibility, I shall refuse to have a share in it, and take the consequences; but, of course, if it is an order from head-quarters, it is a different matter; as in such case I suppose it to have been found necessary to adopt that policy. He ordered me, if separated from him, to burn all the planters' houses I came across."

He insisted that he was "perfectly ready to burn any place which resists, and gives some reason for such a proceeding." But he said, "It seems to me barbarous to turn women and children adrift in that way; and if I am only assisting Colonel Montgomery in a private enterprise of his own, it is very distasteful to me."

He concluded by saying, "I am aware that this is not a military way of getting information, and I hope you will feel that I shall not be hurt if you refuse to answer my question."[5]

Apparently, Halpine never answered Colonel Shaw's letter. In fact, the day after Shaw wrote the letter Halpine left Hilton Head with General Hunter and there is no certainty that the letter ever reached him. While the young colonel waited in vain for an answer he had time enough to write lengthy letters to his mother and sisters and to his wife Annie as well as to Colonel Halpine and Governor Andrew. What time was not spent in letter writing was used in walking about the countryside. Among the places he visited was one of the plantations which had belonged to Pierce Butler before he sold it and its slaves to cover heavy gambling debts and losses sustained in the panic of 1857. As he walked over the plantation that had belonged to Fanny Kemble's ex-husband he found, even then, some of it still beautiful. Among the surroundings which had been so familiar to the English actress he recalled the vehemence with which she had condemned slavery, the talks they had had on the subject when she visited his Boston home, and again when they had met in Sorrento the summer he and his parents were together on the Bay of Naples. But with all the abolitionist influence in his life and in spite of his feeling of

---

[4]Shaw to Andrew, June 14, 1863. Massachusetts Historical Society, *Proceedings,* XIX, 25.

[5]Emilio, p. 44. Quoted in part in *Harper's Weekly,* Sept. 3, 1870.

rightness in the cause for which he was leading his Negro troops he could not justify the cruel and ruthless work of Colonel Montgomery, whose orders he felt had to be obeyed. He wrote to Annie saying, "There was not a deed performed . . . which required any pluck or courage."[6]

In another letter to his mother written on June 22, Colonel Shaw told her how Montgomery had returned from Hilton Head that morning and had found General Quincy Gillmore, who had relieved General Hunter, "very friendly and anxious to second him in every way, with the exception of the burning business." He closed by saying, "Montgomery now tells me that he acted entirely under orders, and was at first very much opposed to it himself, but finally changed his mind."[7]

If it were true that Montgomery was obeying the orders of his superior then it seems to fix the responsibility upon General Hunter. In any case, it tends to relieve Shaw of the guilt. But here, again, one can draw such a conclusion only if the statement is assumed to be true. However, there is little reason to think that Shaw had any intention of misleading his mother concerning his part in the affair.

Colonel Shaw wrote to his mother again on June 28, saying: I think now, as I did at the time of the burning of Darien, that such wanton destruction is cruel, barbarous, impolitic, and degrading to ourselves and our men; and I shall always rejoice that I expressed myself just as I did. . . . It is rather hard that my men, my officers, and myself should have to bear part of the abuse for that affair, when they—the officers, at least—all felt exactly as I did about it.[8]

Others shared Shaw's resentment. Some of the officers back at Hilton Head took up the quarrel and some Northern Abolitionists believed, as Shaw believed, that the Fifty-Fourth was sent to the South to fight for freedom not to pillage, plunder, and burn private homes. Senator Sumner began to get letters protesting Montgomery's behavior. Colonel Higginson said "indiscriminate burning and pillaging is savage warfare [which] demoralizes the soldiers—and must produce a reaction against arming the Negroes." Horace Greeley, of the New York *Tribune*, was concerned about it and sought an explanation. James Thompson, of the Beaufort *Free South*, although of strong abolitionist sentiments, admitted that Montgomery's acts were "irregular" and said they had given the Negro soldiers a bad reputation.[9]

[6]Quoted in Burchard, 109.

[7]Robert Shaw to Sarah Shaw, June 22, 1863.

[8]*Harper's Weekly*, Sept. 3. 1870.

[9]See Rose, 253.

VIII

OMNIA RELINQUIT

It Was not long after the burning of Darien that Shaw and his Negroes had an opportunity to meet the foe head-on. This was the colonel who had said he did not want to attack and destroy defenseless villages but would be willing, "perfectly ready" in fact, to take his troops against any place that showed resistance. The chance to prove the mettle of the black soldiers came in the middle of July in a federal assault on Fort Wagner in Charleston harbor. The fort was on Morris Island protecting the harbor on the Southeast side. This was the Fifty-Fourth's chance to fight against odds, to attack a strongly fortified battery, to strike a manly blow for freedom. This they could do without the shame experienced at Darien; and if they fought bravely they would make of themselves heroes worthy of the name soldier.

Montgomery, leaving Shaw in command of the brigade on St. Simons, went to Hilton Head to get orders from General Quincy Gillmore, their new commander. He returned on June 23 aboard the *Harriet A. Weed* with instructions to move the brigade to Charleston harbor. An incident en route confirmed Shaw's low estimation of the Kansas Jayhawker's character. One of the soldiers on board the *Ben De Ford* failed to observe silence after taps and Montgomery pulled his pistol and calmly shot him. He only wounded him, but in discussing the incident with Shaw later he said he had intended to kill him and toss the body into the ocean. Then again, after transferring the brigade to Port Royal where it encamped while en route to Morris Island Robert was to have another example of Montgomery's cruelty. On a terribly stormy Sunday evening when tents were blown down and a man was killed, one of the Negro soldiers was caught in an attempt to desert. Montgomery, without court-martial, had him summarily shot.[1]

Colonel Shaw was anxious for his regiment to be given a chance to prove to the world that Negro soldiers would fight. He wrote to Brigadier General George C. Strong, who would command the assault on Wagner, requesting permission for the Fifty-Fourth to lead the attack and thus prove the bravery of its men.

An earlier opportunity had come on the eve of the attack at Wagner. It was a diversionary demonstration on James Island. When the drummer sounded the long roll, Wilkie James,[2] Shaw's adjutant, rode along the line ordering the men to fall in; and Shaw, with sword unsheathed, ordered the main body of the regiment into position to await the attack. They stood their ground and thwarted the Confederates. This pleased Shaw's superiors and increased the colonel's confidence in his black soldiers. General Alfred H. Terry, Shaw's division commander, sent word that he was "exceedingly pleased" by the way the Fifty-Fourth conducted itself.[3]

Gillmore wanted to hit Sumter with his big guns, but Fort Wagner was in his way. He had already been beaten back in an attempted invasion on July 10. Now he was determined to try again. He made a successful landing on the island and set the time for the attack at early evening July 18.

As soon as the Fifty-Fourth landed, Shaw, with Wilkie James his adjutant riding beside him, reported to General Strong. He found Strong receptive to his idea of having the Negro regiment lead the attack. So, it was agreed. The Fifty-Fourth had thinned out to six hundred fatigued and hungry men. Nevertheless, Wilkie James remembered that Shaw's face brightened as he

---

[1] Both of these incidents are related by Burchard, pp. 113, 115.

[2] Garth Wilkinson James, brother of William and Henry James, was a strong Abolitionist with no sympathy whatever for the South. After the assassination of Lincoln he wrote his father saying, "You no doubt see something a great deal higher and better than I do in this murder, yet I see something a good deal higher than I ever thought I should. I see God's wise Providence and justice ridding the sinner of a too pure-minded and clement judge, and putting over him a less worthy and more competent and timely one. He knew that Lincoln never would give the hell to these men that they had been preparing themselves for, and consequently arranged this aright." Edmund Wilson, *Patriotic Gore; Studies in the Literature of the American Civil War* (New York, 1962), pp. 237-238.

[3] Dudley Taylor Cornish, *The Sable Arm: Negro Troops in The Union Army, 1861-1865* (New York, 1956), p. 152.

turned to him and ordered him to go back and tell Ned Hollowell, his lieutenant colonel, to bring up the regiment.[4]

Among the defenders of the fort, commanded by Brigadier General William B. Taliaferro, were the First South Carolina, the Sixty-Third Georgia, the Thirty-First North Carolina, the Fifty-First North Carolina, and the Charleston Battalion.[5] Union troops participating in the attack, in addition to Shaw's regiment, were the Sixth and Seventh Connecticut, the Ninth Maine, the Third and Seventh New Hampshire, the Forty-Eighth and One Hundredth New York, the Sixty-Second and Sixty-Seventh Ohio, and the Seventy-Sixth Pennsylvania.[6]

The advance upon the fort began early in the evening as planned. Colonel Shaw was sure his colored troops would bring honor to their state and country and play their proper role in the liberation of their brothers. Had he not promised Governor Andrew this when he accepted the regimental flag from him?

The glow of the setting sun was beginning to fade as a heavy sea fog gathered to make obscure the earthworks of Fort Wagner. Looking more mature than his twenty-five years because of his mustache and chin whiskers and his serious countenance, the young colonel was composed; but "his cheeks were pale and the corners of his mouth twitched slightly" as he gave the command . . .

"Attention"![7]

The familiar voice of their commander rolled out across the sand dunes of Morris Island, and the colored troops sprang to their feet. Then came the order to move forward in quick time until within a hundred yards of the fort, then . . .

"Double quick, and charge!"[8]

The Confederates had seen the formation and were ready. Guns from Sumter, Sullivan's Island, and James Island all began to pour their shells into the path of the advancing regiment, but the Fifty-Fourth marched on with bayonets fixed. Colonel Shaw was forced to dismount to lead the charge and

---

[4]Burchard, p. 133.

[5]Clement A. Evans, editor, *Confederate Military History* (Atlanta, 1899), V, 236.

[6]Frederick H. Dyer, *A Compendium of the War of the Rebellion* (New York and London, 1959), II, 833.

[7]Emilio, p. 79. Compare Saunders Redding, "Tonight for Freedom," *American Heritage,* June, 1958, pp. 52-55, 90.

[8]*Ibid.*

some of the men were forced to wade water up to their knees through the rolling breakers.

Suddenly, Wagner became "a mound of fire, from which issued a stream of shot and shell."[9] Still the troops marched on toward the parapet, not firing a shot but simply pressing their charge in obedience to their colonel's command. An observer said, "The enemy . . . opened upon them furiously with grape canister and a continuous fusillade of small arms. The gallant men, however, plunged on regardless of this murderous reception." Many of them crossed the ditch, wading four feet of water, and gained the parapet.[10] According to Captain Luis Emilio, one of Shaw's officers, the Thirty-First North Carolina "lost heart."[11] In his opinion, had it not been for that fact, it is doubtful whether or not any of Shaw's troops could have reached the parapet. The Massachusetts Negroes stumbled on through sand and water and over the rocks. "A sheet of flame, followed by a running fire, like electric sparks, swept along the parapet, as the Fifty-First North Carolina gave a direct, and the Charleston Battalion a left-oblique, fire."[12] The Negro soldiers began to fall in increasing numbers, but an officer said "the only response the Fifty-Fourth made to the deadly challenge was to change step . . . double quick."[13] Before the regiment reached the parapet many Negroes had fallen; but those still on foot with hot, panting breath had charged the rampart, Colonel Shaw leading and urging them on.

There had been nothing heroic in the capture and destruction of Darien, undefended as it was, but at Wagner courage was tested to the utmost in what proved to be one of the bloodiest engagements of the war. Perhaps, one might say, the belief that the Confederates would shoot them if they surrendered made the Negroes fight with reckless abandon. Be that as it may, the fact remains that they fought with stubborn courage and did not turn and run.

Colonel Shaw gained the rampart and paused on its summit for a moment with raised sword, shouting:

"Forward, Fifty-Fourth!"

Then he fell inside the fort, mortally wounded with a bullet through his heart. More than two hundred of his regiment died with him that night, four-score of them fighting hand to hand around their dead colonel's body until

---

[9]*Ibid.*

[10]*The New York Times,* July 27, 1863.

[11]Emilio, 80.

[12]*Ibid.*

[13]*Ibid.*

each one lay dead beside him.[14] In the words of Confederate General Roswell S. Ripley, "the carnage of the enemy in the confined space in front of Battery Wagner was extreme. The ditch and glacis were encumbered with the slain of all ranks and colors."[15]

News of Colonel Shaw's death was a great shock to his wife and family. Annie sent small Bibles neatly bound in morocco of various colors to the survivors of the regiment. Sarah brooded over her son's death. Surely she must have found some comfort in picturing him in his moment of glory, as the flash of fire would have outlined his body against the blackness. In her imagination she could see him clad in his close-fitting officer's jacket with the silver eagle insignia on each shoulder; see him dressed in his light blue trousers, narrow silk sash around his waist. She could picture the field officer's sword of English make upraised as he ordered the charge.[16] That was the way she would have pictured him. She gloried in his heroism, and in her imagination she must have had him dress the part. She loved his dress uniform and had tried, though in vain, to get him to wear it at his wedding. Actually, the young colonel was dressed in less glamorous fashion for this attack. A correspondent for the *Providence Journal* observed that he was wearing a "simple suit, hardly a uniform, ..."[17]

The Union officers had a high regard for the young colonel. They renamed one of the captured batteries "Fort Shaw," and they said the Confederates had unconsciously honored him when they buried him with his Negroes who had died with him. Later, General Gillmore offered to recover the body and have it shipped home, but the dead colonel's parents requested that it be left with those who had fallen with him. In time, the sea cut away the trench that had been his tomb, and his bones and those of his men were finally washed out into the purifying salty Atlantic.

General George H. Gordon, who had been Shaw's commander in the Shenandoah Valley, expressed sadness and disappointment at the failure of the Fifty-Fourth's assault on Wagner. He said, "In vain, alas! in vain, did brave soldiers stumble from one impediment to another, groping from ditch to parapet, falling by scores beneath the murderous fire of the foe, or mangled by torpedoes under the sands . . . ."[18]

---

[14]See Beauregard to Cooper, July 21, 1863. *OR: Armies*, ser. 1, vol. 28, pt. 2, p. 214.

[15]*OR: Navies*, ser. 1, vol. 14, p. 721.

[16]This is in substance as Emilio describes Shaw's uniform. Emilio, p. 78.

[17]Quoted in *Magazine of History* (Poughkeepsie and Tarrytown, New York, 1914), XIX, 27.

[18]George Henry Gordon, *A War Diary of Events in the War of the Great Rebellion*, 1863-1865 (Boston, 1882), p. 187.

So, there they lay, "white and colored, named and nameless, side by side." In this manner General Gordon expressed his sense of frustration, concluding with the thought that "Save that the grandeur, the sublimity of these deaths raised the colored man to a higher plane of manhood, and weakened the shackles of slavery all over the world, we had gained nothing."[19] Nevertheless, Emerson, poet and essayist, immortalized the brave Colonel's deed with these familiar lines:

> So near is grandeur to our dust,
> So near is God to man,
> When duty whispers low, *thou must*,
> The youth replies, I can.

The failure at Fort Wagner was temporary. On September 6 the Federals forced the Confederate defenders of Wagner to evacuate the fort. Here the Union officers again manifested the spirit of revenge. A South Carolina historian says they brought six hundred Confederate officers from Fort Delaware prison to Morris Island and "confined them under Confederate fire." But he points out that the action was "in retaliation for the keeping of Federal prisoners in Charleston after its . . . bombardment began."[20] As the months wore on, the tide finally turned in favor of Union victory and the freedom that Shaw's troops fought for on the night of July 18, 1863, was finally won.

Victory was bought at the price of death and broken bodies. It was no less costly for the defeated South. Actually, the price of defeat for the South was much higher than the price of victory for the North. Typical of the Southern scene was Frances Butler's description of her father's home near Darien on Butler's Island. Frances returned to the island home with her father, Pierce Butler, in the spring of 1866 to find the floors bare, the window panes out, plaster falling from the walls and ceiling, and a table and "two old chairs" the only furniture. "It was pretty desolate," she confessed to a friend in a letter written on April 12.[21] Yet across the bar at Darien most of the homes were mere rubble. The commanding general at Hilton Head reported finding not "a single human being" at Darien on April 11, 1865, almost two years after the destruction of the town! General Gillmore sent Major J. O. C. Gray, Jr. there to arrange for an exchange of prisoners. Major Gray found the town desolate and unpopulated. General Gillmore's statement that Gray "failed to discover

---

[19]*Ibid.*

[20]David D. Wallace, *The History of South Carolina* (New York, 1934), III, 186n.

[21]Frances Butler Leigh, *Ten Years on a Georgia Plantation Since the War* (London, 1883), 18.

a single human being" is assuredly an exaggeration, but it suggests how thoroughly the Negro troops carried out Colonel Montgomery's orders to burn the town.[22]

Something of the fire and spirit and determination of her mother characterized Frances Butler, but in her ability to work with the plantation Negroes she was more like her father. To the delight of her father, Frances and her little German maid went to work and "put up some curtains". She made them out of white muslin which she had intended to use for petticoats. After having the windows mended, she hung a "picture of General Lee over the mantlepiece," and put her "writing things and nicknacks on the table . . ."[23]

The things made by nature had been less disturbed than structures made by human hands. Frances took pleasure in the "superb magnolia tree, covered with its queenly flowers." Roses were running "in every direction." Orange, fig, and peach trees were in bloom and "every tree and bush [was] alive with red-birds, mocking-birds, black-birds, and jays." As she sat on the piazza a breeze came up "laden with sweet smells and sounds of all descriptions."[24]

Her beloved General Lee himself came to Darien in the spring of 1869, the year before he died. Pale and wan and in poor health the tired warrior, who had worn out in sixty-three years, was on his way to visit his father's grave on Cumberland Island. He was a passenger on the *Lizzie Baker*, a boat operating between Darien and Savannah. He consented to an informal reception on board when the boat stopped at Darien. The news of his arrival spread rapidly and the enthusiastic people from all around crowded the boat, the dock, and even the town, bringing flowers and expressions of esteem to the revered leader of the Lost Cause.[25]

---

[22]Gillmore to Dahlgren, in *OR: Armies,* ser. II, vol. 8, p. 488.

[23]Leigh, p. 19. Fanny Kemble's daughter probably had the privilege of seeing the much-loved Confederate general three years later when he visited Darien.

[24]*Leigh,* p. 20.

[25]Helen S. Barclay, "Short Sketch of McIntosh County, Ga.", September, 1895.

IX

RECONCILIATION

Five Years after the war ended and seven years after her son's death, Sarah Shaw sat one day in her North Shore home near the boat landing at Sailor's Snug Harbor in the town of New Brighton on Staten Island. She was reading the *New York World*.[1] In it was a plea for financial assistance to help the people of St. Andrew's parish at Darien to restore their house of worship. It was signed by the Reverend Robert F. Clute, and his senior warden, William Robert Gignilliat. Sarah had followed intensely through her son's letters the events of that June day seven years before when the church had gone up in flames in the destruction of Darien. And after Robert died at Fort Wagner she had kept and treasured his letters. They were tangible bits to give more substance to memory.

As she scanned the *World*, suddenly a sentence stood out vividly upon the page: "On June 11, 1863, without an engagement, the town of Darien, Georgia, was taken and burned by the United States Colored troops, Colonel Shaw, Fifty-Fourth Massachusetts Regiment, commanding."[2]

The way it came to be published that Colonel Shaw had been in command

---

[1] Mrs. Shaw mentioned the *World* in connection with the placing of blame for the burning of Darien upon Colonel Shaw. This reference was in a letter of Sept. 24, 1870, to the Rev. Clute.

[2] As quoted in *Harper's Weekly,* Sept. 3, 1870.

at Darien was a statement made by a citizen of the town in a letter written to a Savannah newspaper.[3] The letter, written the day after the burning, told how in searching among the ruins the Darien citizen had found an old ledger[4] in which were written the names of the officers presumed to be responsible for the deed. Shaw's name was on the list.

Mrs. Shaw went hastily to her desk to write the editor of *Harper's Weekly* asking him to aid her in correcting what she knew to be a grievous error. She knew her son had not ordered the burning of the town and she was determined to set the record straight. The editor was cooperative and published excerpts from Colonel Shaw's letters of protest which he had written to Governor Andrew and also his letter to Colonel Halpine asking if General Hunter had ordered the burning.[5] It is quite evident, as shown by the fact that General Hunter's order was directed to Montgomery, that the older colonel was in command of the expedition. That fact would not relieve Shaw from whatever guilty conscience might have troubled him, but according to military regulations the officer in command has to accept all responsibility. Montgomery could not possibly have unloaded the blame upon Shaw even if Shaw had not protested. An officer in command can delegate authority but he cannot delegate responsibility. In line with this principle Montgomery's superior could have received an official reprimand. Lincoln had spared General Hunter a reprimand, but had ordered his removal.

Setting the record straight in *Harper's Weekly* was one thing, but Sarah could not be satisfied until she had won the Darien people over to her side and proved to them that Robert should not be condemned for something that Colonel Montgomery had led her son into against his better judgment. She was convinced by Robert's letters that he should not be blamed for something which should more properly rest on the conscience of others. She was determined to persuade the people down on the Georgia coast to see her point of view and thus lessen the hate in their hearts for her dead boy. And if successful she would respond to the appeal for aid in building a new sanctuary. She would make a contribution and also solicit aid from members of her family.

Several motives could have prompted her action. She must have desired to restore that which had been destroyed, although she denied any suggestion of

---

[3] *Daily Morning News* (Savannah), June 16, 1863.

[4] E. Merton Coulter says the ledger was found in the steam mill of Collins and Shine. See Coulter's treatment of the affair under the title, "Robert Gould Shaw and the Burning of Darien, Georgia," *Civil War Magazine* (Dec., 1959).

[5] *Harper's Weekly,* Sept. 3, 1870.

guilt. Of course she wished to defend her dead son's honor and to establish a sort of memorial to his memory. Such a memorial as a church would not bear his name but would be a tangible reminder of her efforts toward reconciliation and a symbol of forgiveness and good will.

On August 29—the year was 1870—she wrote to the Reverend Clute, the rector. If her son had lived she was "confident that he would have wished to contribute to the good work you have in hand, and I shall be much pleased to carry out what I know would be his wish, if I can be assured by you that such action on my part will not be looked upon as a reparation, for we hold our son quite blameless in the matter, as I am sure you will when you read his letters."[6]

The minister hastened to reply. He also released statements to the newspapers which helped to clear the matter in the eyes of the public. Mrs. Shaw then began to contact members of her family in New York and Boston, asking them to assist in the restoration of St. Andrew's.

In the meantime William Gignilliat, the senior warden, wrote to *Harper's*. The letter, written at Darien on September 9, found favor with the editor and he published it in the very next issue of his journal. Gignilliat felt that the editor not only had made out a clear case of the Colonel's blamelessness, but also of his abhorrence of the act, "which now seems, by these extracts, to be fixed upon General Hunter and Colonel Montgomery."

He went on to say that his purpose "was simply to set forth, in as concise a manner as possible, the sad historical fact of the destruction of the town, including church and academy and the other grounds upon which assistance was asked. It was not intended to reflect, even by implication, upon the memory of any one."

Gignilliat explained how he had been misled by a card found in an old mill left standing after the fire on which was printed Shaw's name and others. This gave him the impression that Colonel Shaw was in command of the expedition. Then he spoke with sympathetic feeling concerning Shaw's death: "But the members of St. Andrew's parish are truly glad that the memory of Colonel Shaw—who certainly proved to the world at Wagner that he was a gallant soldier, even as these published fragments of his letters evince him to have been a Christian gentleman—has been exculpated from the disgrace of burning a defenseless town, which contained only old men, women, and children, who were then, while they stood around the smouldering ruins of their homes, finally shelled from the river."

---

[6]Sarah Shaw to Robert Clute, Aug. 29, 1870. Typed copies in possession of Thomas H. Gignilliat, Savannah, Ga. Original lost (see Preface).

He closed with a plea: "Will not Northern friends, taking the simple appeal of the members of the parish in connection with this expression of opinion, deem the rebuilding of St. Andrew's Church a fit subject for their generosity, and act upon the feeling?"[7]

The editor wished to cooperate. He let his readers know that they might send subscriptions to the senior warden or to the rector, or to the Bishop of Georgia, the Right Reverend John W. Beckwith.

Although Robert had never joined a church, the thought that Mr. Gignilliat considered him "a Christian gentleman" pleased Mrs. Shaw. In later correspondence with the rector she assured him that she knew her son to have a "sincerely religious nature."[8]

On September 19, she wrote the rector again: "I hasten to thank you sincerely in my husband's name and my own for your kind letter received yesterday. The little notice from the *Morning News* is very satisfactory. We had seen it, as the proprietor of that paper generously sent it to us. Had you known our son you would understand why all his friends hastened to shield his memory. He died after twenty-five years of a fine and lovely life and left only sweet memories behind him."[9]

She wrote again on the twenty-fourth saying, "I have now great pleasure in enclosing a check for $500.00 and I think I can promise the same amount again before the new year. To show you the same spirit in which the enclosed sum has been given, I quote from a note from my nephew, 'I gladly enclose $100.00 and thank you for asking me.' An aunt of my son writes, 'I enclose my $100.00 with great pleasure. It makes me happy to send it. I feel as if for the first time we have a chance to do something for dear Robert. I am sure he would rejoice in our sending help to the pretty little place which he evidently looked upon with so much pity as it lay desolate before him'."

The mother's desire for reconciliation was strong: "You see, my dear sir, how he was beloved in his family, and how glad we are that his dear name shall not be hated at the South."

The rector's heart was touched as he read the next lines: "Will you excuse me for sending you a very poor photograph but a good likeness, of my son? It is a diminished copy of a fine one taken three months before he died. I want you to see how little likely he would be to do a cruel deed."[10]

---

[7]The full text of the letter is in *Harper's Weekly,* Oct.1, 1870.

[8]Sarah Shaw to Robert Clute, Feb. 4., 1871. Gignilliat Collection.

[9]Sarah Shaw to Robert Clute, Sept. 19, 1870. Gignilliat Collection.

[10]Sarah Shaw to Robert Clute, Sept. 24, 1870. Gignilliat Collection.

In closing she asked about the progress the Darien people were making in their efforts to restore their town. Her question could truthfully have been answered in the negative, for the white citizens hardly had the courage to return immediately from the Ridge which continued to be their refuge during the five years following the war. The blacks were in such large majority in Darien during that period that it could be called a Negro town. In fact, it was under the rule of a Negro Carpetbagger by the name of Tunis G. Campbell. This Black King of Darien came in on a wave of Carpetbaggers who flooded the area. About the time of the burning of Darien General Saxton had put him on Hilton Head Island to help his black brothers settle on abandoned farms. After the fall of Charleston in February, 1865, Campbell took advantage of General William Tecumseh Sherman's order which gave the Negroes temporary possession of abandoned lands on the islands and as far as thirty miles inland.[11] He had set himself up as Governor of St. Catherines and other islands as well as the mainland, a zone defined in Sherman's order.[12] Campbell was evicted by General Davis Tillson, who succeeded Saxton and directed the work of helping Negroes possess abandoned lands in the area under the jurisdiction of the Freedmen's Bureau.

In 1867, that "boisterous and arrogant" Negro had built himself a home in Darien and set himself up as King of the Delta. As a justice of the peace he had carried on a virtual reign of terror in McIntosh County. He had also played a role at the Radical Constitutional Convention of 1868 in Atlanta. He had gotten himself elected to the Radical Georgia Senate, defeating his white opponent by a wide margin. The defeated white candidate was none other than Robert Gignilliat, the senior warden of St. Andrew's.

Of course not all the Negroes in and around Darien followed or obeyed Campbell and the Carpetbaggers; nor was there intense hatred between all members of the two races. Indeed, the white people were so conditioned by the traumatic experience of the war and the destruction of their town that they wanted to put war and hate behind them. It is said by those who know the Darien people and their history that they were so anxious to put it all behind them that few of them related stories of the burning to their children, and few of their descendants ever heard of the Negro Tunis Campbell and his cohorts. Even peace between the races was not unknown in all quarters. This goes back to ante-bellum days when free Negroes such as Roman Gary and his family worshipped with their white friends in pastor Goulding's church. During the time of the rule of Campbell there were some intelligent Negroes who

---

[11] William Tecumseh Sherman, *Memoirs* . . . . (Bloomington, 1957) II, 250-52.

[12] E. Merton Coulter, "Tunis G. Campbell, Negro Reconstructionist in Georgia," Part I, *Georgia Historical Quarterly,* Vol. LI. No. 4 (Dec, 1967), 401-24.

exercised good judgment in handling the governmental affairs of the county that had disfranchised most of the whites, and there were Negroes who held public office after the balance of power had swung to the conservative white Democrats. Such exceptions to the general rule show that some of the people were willing to forgive and were anxious to let the past be forgotten. The Shaw family would find the parishioners of St. Andrew's not resentful but thankful for help from the mother of the colonel who helped burn their town. Gratitude would be the response of those who received her gifts.

Thanks to Mrs. Shaw's efforts, a total of fourteen hundred dollars was received in response to St. Andrew's call for help. The Reverend Clute and his forty-four parishioners went to work immediately to build a modest little chapel on the Ridge. The building was completed and ready for consecration by May, 1871. When first built it was a plain, square, wooden structure with a high-pointed roof. Steps entered directly into the large square room, and the windows were of plain glass. Later, a porch was added, stained-glass windows put in, and the east end of the building made semicircular to provide for an enlarged chancel.

Such response as Sarah Shaw gave to an appeal from the South was a beginning toward the healing of the nation—only a small beginning, to be sure, but a beginning nevertheless. A responding symbol of diminishing hate was seen four years later in a gesture made by some South Carolinians. When Massachusetts celebrated the centennial of the Battle of Lexington to commemorate the beginning of the American Revolutionary War, ex-Confederates from Charleston returned one of the flags which they had captured from Colonel Shaw's regiment at Fort Wagner.[13] The veterans of the dead colonel's old regiment received it, recalling the pride with which he had accepted it. They remembered how he had spoken eloquently of his hope that the emblem would never be dishonored. Thus the seeds of reconciliation were beginning to bear fruit and gradually people like Unionists of Hampton, Virginia, would remember less vividly the burning of their town and the smoldering fire of hate would die down in the breasts of Rebels who had lost their property at Darien, while up North the wheels of industry turned and the rich blood of commerce flowed, and out in Kansas the grain farmers prospered, and money talk became the absorbing topic of former Abolitionists.

Within a year after the chapel on the Ridge was consecrated the congregation of St. Andrew's began to make plans for a new sanctuary in Darien. They built it on the site of the old Bank of Darien near the spot where

---

[13]See Hodding Carter, *The Angry Scar* (New York, 1969), p. 345.

the original edifice had stood until that awful day when Black invaders put the torch to it. It was built along the style of rural English churches, the plans having been brought over by the Right Reverend J. W. Leigh, the husband of Frances Butler. By the end of the decade the building was completed and in use. The little chapel on the Ridge was sold to the Baptists and the brass cross, brass vases, and other altar pieces were placed in the Darien church while other furnishings were given to the Negroes for their use in St. Cyprian's nearby.

The chapel on the Ridge was later destroyed by fire and no physical trace of Mrs. Shaw's memorial to her son remained. But in 1897 a lasting memorial, the work of Augustus Saint-Gaudens, was placed on Boston Common. The unveiling of the Shaw Memorial inspired a New England poet to write:

> He and his dusky braves
> So faint of glorious graves!—
> One instant stood, and then
> Drave through the cloud of purple steel and flame,
> Which wrapped him, held him, gave him not again,
> But in its trampled ashes left to Fame
> An everlasting name![14]

The bronze monument shows a mass of figures framed between Ionic-capped columns. These columns support the arched dome. Colonel Shaw, astride his horse, is more prominent than the other figures. His black soldiers are marching in close formation with their packs and blanket rolls on their backs and their long rifles on their shoulders. The drummer boy leads the troops as the guardian angel hovers over them. Above the angel are these words:

OMNIA RELINQUIT SERVARE REPUBLICAM

Following the unveiling, memorial exercises were held in Music Hall. An oration by William James was followed by an address by Booker T. Washington, an ex-slave who had risen to the position of a Southern educator and whose philosophy of life is now engraved upon his own monument at Tuskegee Institute in Alabama: "No man, black or white, from North or South, shall drag me down so low as to make me hate him."

No such monument as the Shaw Memorial was ever erected to Colonel Montgomery, the fighting parson who learned hate on Kansas plains. By the time the Shaw Memorial was erected in Boston, even the memory of the

---

[14]From "An Ode on the Unveiling of the Shaw Memorial on Boston Common, May Thirty-First, 1897," by Thomas Bailey Aldrich.

Kansas Jayhawker was fading. Colonel Montgomery had died the very first day of 1871, the year[15] that the congregation of St. Andrew's began to worship in the chapel made possible by the benevolence of the Shaw family. Some of the Southern Negroes freed by the Kansas colonel were among those who remembered him, for they had followed their liberator to his Western home. Whether or not the Negroes' memory of their old colonel was an affectionate one is not on record. But the gratitude of the Darien people for Northern help was strengthened as they met for worship Sunday after Sunday in the peaceful little chapel on the Ridge and later in their church in Darien.

As the St. Andrew's parishioners continued to worship in the tranquil atmosphere of their river town they were conditioned spiritually so that they had a will to live. Purpose replaced frustration, and they were strengthened in their determination to overcome the great calamity that had befallen them. They resolved to rebuild their town. In the act of worship there was kindled a hope within them, and with it a faith in themselves and a renewed confidence that now through their own efforts they could bring life and vitality to their community. In this spirit other groups rebuilt their churches; and they, too, caught the enthusiasm and optimism of the parishioners of St. Andrew's. It would be incorrect to say hope had completely died in the hearts of the people of Darien. Even as they had viewed the smoking ruins of their burned homes they had not despaired altogether. From the time the remnant of the three companies of men who marched away in 1861 came back from the war, hope grew stronger. That remnant was small—less than fifty returned. Some of them were amputees or carried lifetime scars of battle, but after what they had been through they were hardened to endure what lay ahead.

Well before the century closed the timber industry had revived and the turpentine business began to bring prosperity to Darien and McIntosh County. Darien reached its high water mark in the eighteen-eighties. Its foreign export offices and customs house gave it an international reach. By 1874 the town again had a newspaper. Emphasis on the timber industry is seen in the name, *Darien Timber Gazette.* Evidence of a return to national loyalty and patriotism appears in a July issue of this paper in 1875. In early dawn on the Fourth the townspeople were awakened by the "belching of the time honored 'thirteen rounds' "; and by noon the streets "were alive with happy faces of every hue and complexion, gladdened by the observance of this National Holiday."

In its issue of January 30, 1880, the *Gazette* announced the reopening of the Magnolia House. This hotel was located on the river front "connecting

---

[15]Montgomery died on Jan. 1, 1871, at the age of 57, Mitchell, p. 30.

with the wharves of the Savannah and Florida steamers."[16] The stores, hotels, and bars became more numerous and the hum of saw mills and the whistle of the steamboats kept the marsh hens and sea gulls excited and disturbed the lazy alligators sunning on the muddy banks of the Darien channel of the Altamaha. And blasts from hunter's guns reminded the ducks that man still held dominion over the earth.

More homes were built, families increased, and the town took on a gay mood. Tom Hilton recalled a "charming society" made up of old English and Scottish families, living together with the more recent arrivals who came and found Darien a delightful place to spend all the remaining days of their years.[17] Tom remembered the big social events of the year, "a Masonic Ball on St. Johns Day, a Military Ball given by the McIntosh Dragoons, and a Fireman's Ball, given by the Volunteer Fire Co." The Hiltons and the Fosters in their beautiful homes on the Ridge always gave one major dance each year. There were "Tilts" followed by a ball where the Queen was crowned by the trooper who had made the best score. The young people often went on excursions up and down the river channels and through the sounds. These excursions were far different from the expeditions of abolitionist colonels with their Negro troops many years before, and now all but forgotten. Favorite places for pleasure trips were Fernandina Beach between St. Marys and Jacksonville, and nearer places such as Frederica on St. Simons Island and Brunswick on the mainland. These excursions were made on a big "lighter" towed by a tugboat and floored over for dancing. Baseball was the favorite team sport for the youth of Darien and was next to hunting and fishing among their recreational activities. The Ridge team would challenge Darien and supporters of both teams would ride to the game in gaily decorated buggies drawn by ribbon-bedecked horses. On holidays the young men with masked faces would ride from house to house fantastically dressed in absurd costumes.[18] At Christmas time the most popular homes were those where the eggnog flowed most freely.

Culture came again to Darien. The young men of the town organized the Altamaha Social Club. Its primary interest was the theatre. On Monday evening, February 2, 1880 they with the help of the ladies planned "a dramatic

---

[16]The *Darien Timber Gazette* began in 1874 with Richard Grubb as editor. A microfilm file is in the University of Georgia Library. The two copies cited for 1880 are deposited in the Emory University Library.

[17]Thomas Hilton, *High Water on the Bar* (Savannah, 1951), p. 19. Actually, there were at that time very few Scottish families remaining in or near Darien, according to Bessie Lewis, an authority on the history of the region.

[18]*Ibid.*

entertainment at their hall [on] the Ridge." The entertainment, as announced, consisted of two "well-known" plays, "Time Tries All" and "The Old Guard."[19] Some citizens of the town reached such a position of affluence that they could get their entertainment and recreation at faraway places. Mayor James Walker was financially able to leave his duties in July, 1881, and take his family to Virginia Springs.[20]

Because life once more had meaning and because the Darien people believed in a Tomorrow, they built those things which the eye could see and strengthened those unseen things of the spirit which helped make a new day for them. In time more homes graced the long vista of marsh land, shrimp boats crowded the river's wharves, and great stores of pine tree products and lumber mounted higher and higher on the docks. Finally, this town, like other brave little towns all over the South, covered up its burned scars of war and out of the cooling ashes of the flame of hate there emerged a new Darien and a new South.

---

[19]*Gazette*, Jan. 30, 1880.
[20]*Gazette*, July 15, 1881.

BIBLIOGRAPHY

I. Primary Sources

A. Unpublished Manuscripts

Barclay, Helen S. "Sketch of McIntosh County," 1895, UDC Records, Darien, Ga.

Darien Presbyterian Church Records, Darien, Ga.

Egmont Papers. In University of Georgia Library, Athens, Ga.

Georgia. Glynn County. Census of 1820. (microfilm)

Georgia. McIntosh County. Census of 1820. (microfilm)

Georgia. Glynn County. Census of 1860. (microfilm)

Georgia. McIntosh County. Census of 1860. (microfilm)

King, Reuben. Journal, 1801-1806. Georgia Historical Society Collection, Savannah, Ga.

Pease, Augusta I. Letter, UDC records, Darien, Ga.

St. Andrews' Episcopal Church Records, Darien, Ga.

Smith, Captain R. A. Letter. In possession of Mrs. Daly Smith, Macon, Ga.

Shaw, Sarah Blake. Letters. Typed copies in possession of Thomas Gignilliat, Savannah, Ga.

Walker, Sarah Amanda King. Account of "Mallow" raid, Nov. 7, 1862. Typed copy in Georgia Historical Society Collection, Savannah, Ga.

B. Newspapers and Magazines

Atlantic Monthly (Boston)
Commonwealth (Boston)
Daily Morning News (Savannah, Ga.)
Darien Gazette (Darien, Ga.)
Darien Phoenix (Darien, Ga.)
Darien Telegraph (no file known to be extant)
Frank Leslie's Illustrated Weekly (New York)
Georgia Historical Quarterly (Athens, Ga.)
Harper's Weekly Magazine (New York)
McIntosh County Herald (Darien, Ga.)
Magazine of History (New York), XIX (1914)
Massachusetts Historical Society, *Proceedings* (Boston), 19, 40, 42.
New York Herald
New York Times
Savannah Republican

C. Books

Bartram, William. *The Travels of William Bartram*. Edited by Mark Van Doren. New York: Dover Publications, 1928. (First published in 1791: Philadelphia, Pa.)

Candler, Allen D. (ed.) *Georgia Colonial Records*. 25 vols. Atlanta: Chas. P. Byrd, state printer, 1904.

Dyer, Frederick H. *A Compendium of the War of the Rebellion*. 3 vols. With a new introduction by Bell I. Wiley. New York: T. Yoseloff, 1959.

Emilio, Luis F. *History of the Fifty-Fourth Regiment of Massachusetts Volunteers Infantry, 1863-1865*. 2d ed. revised. Boston: The Boston Book Co., 1894.

Evans, Clement A. (ed.) *Confederate Military History* [12 vols.], Vol. 5. Atlanta: Confederate Publishing Co., 1899.

Georgia Historical Society. *Index to United States Census of Georgia for 1820*. Savannah, 1963.

Gordon, George Henry. *A War Diary of Events in the War of the Great Rebellion, 1863-1865*. Boston: J. R. Osgood and Co., 1882.

Hall, Margaret Hunter. *Mrs. Basil Hall. The Aristocratic Journey; being the outspoken letters of Mrs. Basil Hall written during a fourteen months sojourn in America, 1827-1828*. Prefaced and edited by Una Pope-Hennessy. New York: D. P. Putnam's Sons, 1931.

Halpine, Charles G. (ed.) *The Life and Adventures, Songs, Services, and Speeches of Private Miles O'Reilly*. New York: Carleton, 1864.

Higginson, Thomas Wentworth. *Army Life in a Black Regiment*. By Thomas Wentworth Higginson, Late Colonel, 1st South Carolina Volunteers. Boston: Fields, Osgood, and Co., 1870.

Hilton, Thomas. *High Water on the Bar*. Savannah, 1951.

House, Albert Virgil, editor. *Planter Management and Capitalism in Ante-Bellum Georgia: The Journal of Hugh Fraser Grant, Ricegrower*. New York: Columbia University Press, 1954.

Kemble, Frances Anne. *Journal of a Residence on a Georgia Plantation in 1838-1839*. New York: Harper and Brothers, 1863.

King, Spencer B., Jr. *Georgia Voices; A Documentary History to 1872*. Athens: University of Georgia Press, 1966.

Leigh, Frances Butler. *Ten Years on a Georgia Plantation Since the War*. London: R. Bentley and Sons, 1883.

Lyell, Charles. *A Second Visit to the United States of North America*. 2 vols. New York: Harper and Bros., 1849.

———, *Travels in North America in the Years 1841-1842.* 2 vols. New York: Wiley and Putnam, 1845.

Matthews, James M. (ed.) *Statutes at Large of the Confederate States of America.* Richmond, 1863.

Moore, Frank (ed.) *Rebellion Record.* 11 vols. and supplement. New York: G. P. Putnam, 1861-1863; H. Holt, 1864; D. Van Nostrand, 1864-1866. (Special collections. University of Ga. Libraries, Athens, Ga.)

Quarterman, Elizabeth Walker. *The Home on the Bluff.* (n.p., n.d.) Bound in with *Reminiscences of a Country Boy.* By Luther H. Quarterman. Drawings by Leonora. (Georgia Historical Collections, Savannah, Ga.)

Sherman, William Tecumseh. *Memoirs of General William T. Sherman.* 2 vols. complete in one. Civil War Centennial Series. Bloomington: Indiana University Press, 1957.

Towne, Laura M. *Letters and Diary of Laura M. Towne written from the Sea Islands of South Carolina, 1862-1884,* ed. by Rupert Sargent Holland. Cambridge: Riverside Press, 1912.

United States. Navy Department. Official Records of the Union and Confederate Navies in the War of the Rebellion. 4 series. Washington, D. C.: Government Printing Office, 1894-1927.

United States. War Department. *The Official Atlas of the Civil War.* Introduction by Henry Steele Commager. (New York, London, Thomas Yoseloff, 1958).

United States. War Department. *The War of the Rebellion: A Compilation of the Official Records of the Union and Confederate Armies.* Published under the direction of the Secretary of War, Four series, 70 vols. in 128. Washington: Government Printing Office, 1880-1901.

Wilson, Edmund. *Patriotic Gore: Studies in the Literature of the American Civil War.* New York: Oxford University Press, 1962.

II. Secondary Sources

A. Books

Bradford, Sarah H. *Harriet, the Moses of Her People.* New York: George R. Lockwood & Sons, 1886.

Burchard, Peter. *One Gallant Rush: Robert Gould Shaw and His Brave Black Regiment.* New York: St. Martin's Press, 1965.

Carse, Robert. *Department of the South: Hilton Head Island in the Civil War.* Columbia, S. C.: The State Printing Co., 1961.

Carter, Hodding. *The Angry Scar.* Garden City, New York: Doubleday Co., 1959.

Castel, Albert. *A Frontier State at War.* Published for the American Historical Association. Ithaca: Cornell University Press, 1958.

Cato, Margaret Davis. *Our Todays and Yesterdays.* Brunswick, Ga.: Glover Bros., 1926.

Conrad, Earl. *Harriet Tubman.* Washington: The Associated Publishers, 1943.

Cornish, Dudley Taylor. *The Sable Arm: Negro Troops in the Union Army, 1861-1865.* New York: Longmans, Green and Co., 1956.

Coulter, E. Merton. *Thomas Spalding of Sapelo.* Baton Rouge: Louisiana State University Press, 1940.

Crane, Verner W. *The Promotion Literature of Georgia.* Cambridge: Harvard University Press, 1925.

———. *The Southern Frontier, 1670-1732.* Ann Arbor: University of Michigan Press, 1956.

Franklin, John Hope. *From Slavery to Freedom.* revised ed. New York: A. Knopf Co., 1967.

Lewis, Bessie Mary. *The Pageant of Darien.* Pamphlet, n.p., 1936.

Lovell, Caroline Couper. *The Golden Isles of Georgia.* Boston: Little Brown and Co., 1932.

Mitchell, William A. *Linn County, Kansas: A History.* Kansas City, Mo., 1928.

Morris, Richard B. (ed.). *Encyclopedia of American History.* New York: Harper, 1953.

Rose, Willie Lee. *Rehearsal for Reconstruction, The Port Royal Experiment.* With an introduction by C. Vann Woodward. Indianapolis: Bobbs-Merrill Co., 1964.

Vanstory, Burnette. *Georgia's Land of the Golden Isles.* Athens: University of Georgia Press, 1956.

Wallace, David D. *The History of South Carolina.* 4 vols. New York: The American Historical Society, Inc., 1934.

Yearns, W. B. *The Confederate Congress.* Athens, Georgia: University of Georgia, 1960.

B. Articles

Coulter, E. Merton. "Robert Gould Shaw and the Burning of Darien, Georgia," *Civil War History,* V, No. 4 (Dec., 1959), 363-73.

Coulter, E. Merton. "Tunis G. Campbell, Negro Reconstructionist in Georgia," Part I, *Georgia Historical Quarterly,* LI, No. 4 (Dec. 1967), 401-24.

Lewis, Bessie Mary, "Darien, a Symbol of Defiance and Achievement," *Georgia Historical Quarterly,* XX (Sept., 1936), 185-98.

Redding, Saunders. "Tonight for Freedom," *American Heritage,* IX, No. 4 (June, 1958), 52-55, 90.

INDEX